Hike and Bike Bowland – Updates and Addenda March 2015

Walk C6, p42. Garstang Super 8 bus service no longer operates.

Walks C9, p55 and **L4, p106.** Bowland Transit B12 bus service no longer operates.

Walk C12, p69. Bowland Transit B10 bus from Clitheroe/Slaidburn, Monday–Friday.

Walk C14, p75. Bus runs summer Sundays and Bank Holidays.

Walks L2, p101 and **L3, p103.** Slaidburn no longer has buses to/from Settle.

Walk L5, p109. Bus B12 no longer operates. Garstang–Preston and Preston–Chipping bus routes intersect at Broughton.

Walk L6, p112. No bus service to Abbeystead.

Ride R1, p118. Refreshments are available at Crook o'Lune (weekends only at low season) and in Caton.

Ride M1, p142. Pubs and café in Hornby.

Ride M2, p146. The trail after point 4 has become a bit more eroded – either harder or more fun depending on your perspective.

Ride M3, pp148–9. There have been major developments in Gisburn Forest and it is now a fully-fledged trail centre. The Cocklet Hill car-park can still be used but there is now a Forest Hub, with a skills loop and café – next to Stephen Park on the map p149. Continue a short way along the road past Cocklet Hill and the access to the Hub is well-signed.

The trails themselves are still mostly as described, although new singletrack sections and a couple of standalone downhill tracks have been added. The start from the Hub uses a new section of singletrack, joining the trails as described before the descent to the causeway. Check maps onsite or online for the latest info: www.forestry.gov.uk/gisburn

Hike and Bike
Bowland

Jon Sparks

First published in 2011 by Grey Stone Books

British Library Cataloguing in Publication Data

A catalogue record of this book is available from the British Library.

Editor: Chris Bagshaw, Little Spider Publishing

Printed in Poland by Polskabook (www.polskabook.co.uk)

ISBN 978-1-902017-03-7

Contains Ordnance Survey Data

While every effort has been taken by the author to ensure the accuracy of this book, changes do occur, and these may affect the contents. Neither the author nor the publisher accepts liability for these.

Hike and Bike Bowland

Jon Sparks

GREY STONE
Books

Acknowledgments

First, thanks to my parents for many things, including moving to a house within striking distance of Clougha Pike when I was at an impressionable age.

Thanks to several teachers, especially Bill Tissington, for opening my eyes to the geography and geology of the area. Thanks to Reg Stoddon and staff at GL Robertson in Lancaster (a proper camera shop), and David Farnell Photo Labs, for much help and advice – even if, in these digital days, I don't see as much of you as I used to. Darren Robins for introducing me to the delights of mountain biking and Ray Mazey and Clare Rawson for any technical ability I may have picked up. Dave Pegg for scary moments on Thorn Crag.

Many people have accompanied me on walks and bike rides in this fabulous area; too many to list them all but special mentions to Lancaster Cycling Club and especially the 'Kellet Wheelers'; Jonathan and Julia Westaway, and Arthur Frank.

Above all, as always, thanks to my partner Bernie Carter for all manner of support, for being the best possible company on many of the walks and rides and for (almost) endless tolerance for my repeated requests to 'just hold it there' and 'just do that bit again'.

For updates to this book and information on other titles please visit the publisher's website at

www.grey-stone.co.uk

Contents

Introduction...11

Circular Walks

Walk C1 Clougha Pike...20
Distance: 8.2km (5.1 miles)
Ascent: 382m (1,255ft)

Walk C2 Tarnbrook and Ward's Stone................................24
Distance: 14.8km (9.2 miles)
Ascent: 517m (1,695ft)

Walk C3 Wyresdale...28
Distance: 6.4km (4 miles)
Ascent: 139m (455ft)

Walk C4 Brennand Great Hill and Wolfhole Crag.............32
Distance: 14.3km (8.9 miles)
Ascent: 485m (1,591ft)
Bonus walk: Black Clough
Distance: 4.6km (2.9 miles)
Ascent: 245m (805ft)

Walk C5 Grizedale Head...37
Distance: 12.4km (7.7 miles)
Ascent: 450m (1,475ft)
Bonus walk: Grizedale Lea
Distance: 4km (2.5 miles)
Ascent: 50m (165ft)

Walk C6 Nicky Nook and Grize Dale..................................42
Distance: 7.3km (4.5 miles)
Ascent: 285m (935ft)

6

Walk C7 Bleasdale...**45**
Distance: 11.5 km (7.1 miles)
Ascent: 430m (1,410ft)

Walk C8 Brock Bottoms and Beacon Fell..**49**
Good things come in small packages
Distance: 8.5km (5.3 miles)
Ascent: 260m (855ft)
Bonus Walk: More Brock Bottoms
2.4km (1.5 miles)
Ascent: 60m (195ft)

Walk C9 Burnslack, Paddy's Pole and Parlick.....................................**55**
Distance: 14.3km (8.9 miles)
Ascent: 545m (1,790ft)

Walk C10 Longridge Fell; a circuit from Hurst Green....................**60**
Distance: 11.6km (7.2 miles)
Ascent: 280m (920ft)

Walk C11 Three Rivers (hunting for hobbits).....................................**64**
Distance: 10.6km (6.6 miles)
Ascent: 175m (575ft)

Walk C12 Hodder Heights and Crag Stones.......................................**69**
Distance: (from Newton Bridge) 10.6km (6.6 miles)
Ascent: 274m (900ft)

Walk C13 Croasdale, upper Whitendale and Dunsop Head..........**72**
Distance: 12.3km (7.6 miles)
Ascent: 570m (1,870ft)

Walk C14 Pendle Hill...**75**
Distance: 11.8km (7.3 miles
Ascent: 490m (1,605ft)

Walk C15 Bolton-by-Bowland and Sawley...**79**
Distance: 9km (5.6 miles)
Ascent: 210m (690ft)

Walk C16 Gisburn Forest, Whelp Stone and Bowland Knotts.........83
Distance: 17.7km (11 miles)
Ascent: 470m (1,540ft)

Walk C17 Roeburndale...88
Distance: 12.9km (8 miles)
Ascent: 420m (1,380ft)

Walk C18 Lawkland Moss...92
Distance: 7.8km (4.8 miles)
Ascent: 145m (475ft)

Long Distance/ Linear Walks..95

L1 Caton–Hornby..97
Distance: 13.4km (8.3 miles)
Ascent: 50m (165ft)

L2 Hornby–Slaidburn...101
Distance: 22.9km (14.2 miles)
Ascent: 695m (2,280ft)

L3 Slaidburn–Clitheroe..103
Distance: 14.5km (9 miles)
Ascent: 365m (1,200ft) Descent: 425m (1,395ft)

L4 Clitheroe–Chipping...106
Distance: 16.2km (10.1 miles)
Ascent: 400m (1,315ft)

L5 Chipping–Garstang..109
Distance: 17.3km (10.8 miles)
Ascent: 355m (1,165ft) Descent: 454m (1,490ft)

L6 Garstang–Caton..112
Distance: 29.6km (18.4 miles)
Ascent: 730m (2,395ft)

Road Bike Rides..116

Ride R1 Lune Valley..118
Distance: 28.2km (17.5 miles)
Ascent: 610m (2,000ft)

Ride R2 Wenning and Hindburn...............................121
Distance: 22.3km (13.9 miles)
Ascent: 415m (1,360ft)

Ride R3 Brock, Bleasdale and Harrisend....................124
Distance: 33.8km (21 miles)
Ascent: 465m (1,525ft)

Ride R4 Chipping–Oakenclough–Trough of Bowland.........127
Distance: 44.6km (27.7 miles)
Ascent: 765m (2,510ft)

Ride R5 Bashall Eaves–Marl Hill–Harrop Fell–Holden.........130
Distance: 39km (24.2 miles)
Ascent: 610m (2,000ft)

Ride R6 Tour de Pendle Hil......................................133
Distance: 30.1km (18.7 miles)
Ascent: 740m (2,430ft)

Ride R7 Bowland Knotts and Cross o'Greet................136
Distance: 45.6km (28.3 miles)
Ascent: 995m (3,265ft)

Mountain Bike Rides...139

Ride M1 Caton Moor..142
Distance: 16.3km (10.1 miles)
Ascent: 494m (1,620ft)

Ride M2 Chipping–Dunsop Bridge and back...............145
Distance: 22.5km (14 miles)
Ascent: 515m (1,690ft)

Ride M3 Gisburn Forest Trails...148
Distance: Bottoms Beck trail 8km (5 miles), The '8' 18km (11.2 miles)

Ride M4 Salter Fell...154
Distance (Out-and-back ride): 42km (26.1 miles)
Ascent: 885m (2,900ft)
Distance (Circuit): 50.2km (31.2 miles)
Ascent: 1,110m (3610ft)

Sources of Information..159

The west top of Ward's Stone

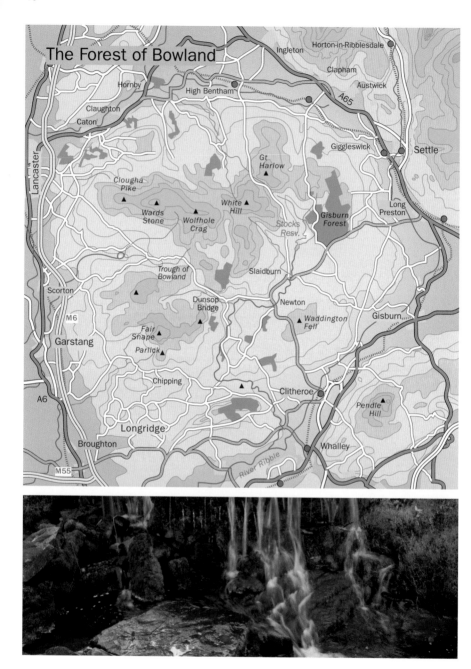

Waterfall in the little valley before the climb to Clougha Pike (Walk C1)

Introduction

Bowland is connoisseurs' country. On first impressions, it's long heathery ridges wrapped around green valleys, but it's a lot more than that. It's wide horizons and tight-knit villages. It's easy striding on a grassy ridge with paragliders wheeling past like giant exotic moths. It's a flounder through knee-deep snow to get a sunset view, and then the electrifying realisation that those razor-sharp outlines are the Carneddau, 120km distant. It's lying back on a warm rock and listening to the bubbling call of the curlew. It's the pleasure of the unexpected: a mossy green clough incised into the edge of a wide dark moor, a wrinkled fist of gritstone suddenly appearing from the endless heather, a hare rocketing from cover a few metres away. It's an easy amble through meadows glowing with buttercups and a white-knuckle ride on the rocky mountain bike trails of Gisburn Forest.

Let the hordes scurry past to the Lakes and Dales; we know there's plenty of pleasure to be found right here. In the absence of the hordes, the pleasure of solitude is one of the chief delights. Apart from a few hotspots – and even those mostly at weekends – Bowland remains relatively quiet. I have often walked for hours without seeing another soul. If you want crowds, you've come to the wrong place.

Background

The Forest of Bowland, by strict definition, is a compact block of upland country including extensive areas of moorland over 400m (1,312ft), with its highest summit at Ward's Stone (561m/1,841ft). Pedants might debate the inclusion of Longridge Fell, separated from the main mass by the valleys of Loud and Hodder, but it is clearly cut from the same cloth. Geographically, there's no question that Pendle Hill is not part of the Forest of Bowland, though it is geologically akin and it does fall under the same Area of Outstanding Natural Beauty (AONB) – and anyway, it's just too good to leave out. The total area of the AONB is 803 sq km (310 sq miles), of which over 90 per cent is in Lancashire; the rest is claimed by North Yorkshire and abuts the Yorkshire Dales National Park.

The word 'Forest' may lead some to expect a heavily wooded area, but that's not what we see today. Small woods abound but larger forests are rare, apart from Gisburn Forest (Lancashire's largest) in the east and a lesser expanse on Longridge Fell. The name actually harks back to an older meaning of the word, an area set aside for hunting, usually by royalty or the nobility. This status, along with the relative infertility of most of the area, helps account for its low population. Today shooting – grouse on the high moors, pheasant on the lower slopes – remains economically important and influences the management of the uplands in particular, sustaining the globally rare and important heather moorland habitat. You might not relish the idea of killing birds in the name of sport, but two facts are inescapable: without the shoots, the landscape would soon look very different; and, without the shoots, many (already scarce) rural jobs would be lost. This is not untouched wilderness – nowhere in England is – but it is country that often feels wild.

In distant views the fells may appear smooth and rounded, but close up they often appear much rockier – never more exuberantly so than on Clougha Pike. A few crags, like Thorn Crag and Cold Stone, have attracted the attention of rock climbers, but there are no really popular climbing grounds to compare with the Peak District. Belying its gloomy reputation, the gritstone of the heights is typically quite light in colour, sometimes glinting silvery in the sunlight, and many of the outcrops are a pleasure to scramble about on.

Underlying the grit, and often outcropping on the lower slopes, is Carboniferous Limestone; this has been extensively quarried around Clitheroe. These lower slopes and valley floors are green and relatively fertile, but dominated by dairy farming rather than arable. It's a landscape of small fields and scattered woods, the essence of Middle England – or even, some say, Middle-earth (see Walk C11).

Bowland is a rich and many-faceted area. I would hardly feel that I knew it properly if I had not explored by bike as well as on foot. To give as wide an experience of Bowland as possible, this book therefore includes walks (both circular and linear) and rides, for both road and mountain bikes. Of course the bike routes could be done on foot as well – though not vice versa. But they are, honestly, easier and more fun by bike.

Practicalities

Bases

There are no large centres of population within the AONB. The largest settlement is the conjoined villages of Caton and Brookhouse on the north western edge of the area, mustering about 4,000 people altogether. Elsewhere the area is thinly populated, but villages such as Slaidburn and Chipping provide the essential amenities such as pubs and cafés. Accommodation is quite sparse, mostly in the form of pub rooms or bed and breakfast. There is a Youth Hostel at Slaidburn (closed in winter, except for pre-booked groups) and there are camping barns at Hurst Green and Chipping, as well as a few small campsites. In this part of the world it is generally best to arrange accommodation in advance rather than just turning up and hoping for the best.

However, the AONB is closely ringed with several towns, and a couple of cities, which provide a much wider range of accommodation and other amenities. The most obvious is *Clitheroe*, a very attractive small town and 'capital' of the Ribble valley, perfectly placed between Bowland proper and the outlier of Pendle Hill. It has direct rail links to Manchester as well as links to Preston, and good bus services into central Bowland and around Pendle Hill. It has outdoor gear shops and a bike shop.

Lancaster is much larger but has several advantages: it's on the West Coast Main Line (as little as 2½ hours from London), close to the M6, has a great range of restaurants and pubs, gear shops and bike shops, and has good bus and rail services to the northern side of Bowland. There is also a good foot- and cycle-path beside the River Lune allowing direct traffic-free access to the Lune valley. This makes it particularly attractive as the start/finish of a longer tour (see the Linear Walks section).

Other towns and villages around the periphery include:

Garstang: pleasant, small market town with some good pubs. Possible direct access to a couple of the walks, but better as a base for several of the road bike rides. Good bus links to Preston and Lancaster.

Scorton: small but popular village just north of Garstang and right on the edge of the AONB. A bit of a honeypot for cyclists.

The Lune valley: attractive valley, good cycling country and access to walks on the northern Bowland fells. The villages of Caton/Brookhouse, Hornby and Wray all have pubs and/or cafés and accommodation.

High Bentham: small town with railway station, pubs, cafés, etc. Good base for several bike rides.

Settle: very tourist-oriented town (on the edge of the Yorkshire Dales National Park) so good facilities, and accessible by rail. It's very close to the boundary of the Bowland AONB but not in fact particularly convenient for most of the walks and rides.

Plan of the book

The book falls into four sections; first are the circular walks (prefix C, i.e. C1 to C19); I've also included a few 'bonus walks' that can easily be tagged on to the main walk as an aperitif or 'afters'. They also allow different options for one group, so that for instance Dad and the younger kid(s) could spend an easy afternoon exploring the secret valley of Grizedale Lea while Mum and the older one(s) go for a longer walk over Grizedale Head (C5 and bonus). Next come the linear walks L1–L6, which can be linked into a continuous tour. These are followed by road bike rides (R1–R7) and finally mountain bike rides (M1–M4).

Timings: Walks

Walks timings are largely based on personal experience and intuition but have been compared against well-tried formulas. Individual walking speeds do vary; these timings are not a target or a cast-iron guarantee, but should provide a reasonable means of comparison between the walks. If, after doing a few of these walks, you find you are consistently faster or slower than the stated times, this can be factored in future. All timings relate only to time spent actually walking and make no allowance for stops, whether for picnics, birdwatching, photography or any other cause. You'll have to make your own judgement as to how much time these will add.

On poorer days there's less temptation to linger; the impulse is always to keep walking. For notes on bike ride timings see intros to the relevant sections.

Equipment: Walks

Footwear

Bowland is not the Alps but some of it is rough, paths can be poor, and wet patches are (to break it to you gently) not unknown. This can apply to many of the valley walks as well as the higher ones. This is generally terrain for boots rather than trainers, and waterproof boots are usually best. These can either be leather (in good condition, treated regularly with Nikwax or similar proofing product) or fabric boots with a waterproof breathable liner such as Gore-Tex. However, it's neither necessary nor pleasurable to lumber yourself with heavy mountain-macho boots; keep it light but not flimsy. In poorer conditions, summer or winter, gaiters can also help to keep the wet and muck out.

Other gear

It's not my place to dictate what you should carry on a walk, but a few points are worth mentioning. Like any hill area, Bowland weather can be changeable, and the tops can be very bare and exposed, so even on the best-looking days it is sensible to carry an extra wind- and water-proof layer. Clean (i.e. drinkable) water is rare on these peaty hills so carry ample supplies of your own. I'm a great believer in hydration packs, which allow you to drink without stopping. On longer walks carry some food too. A basic first-aid kit is also a sensible inclusion. Camera, binoculars, bird book, wild flower book... the list could go on.

Navigation

Navigation in Bowland can be tricky, compared to areas such as the Lake District where there are rather more well-used paths, and ridges are also mostly well-defined. If things go wrong it can be a serious business as you can be a long way from roads or even decent tracks, with few other walkers around. Though navigational instructions in this volume are fairly detailed, it's very difficult to give a set of instructions guaranteed to get you off Brennand Great Hill if a thick mist or blizzard descends suddenly.

Maps

A map is invaluable for several reasons. It puts the route itself in a wider context and also gives a much better chance of locating yourself if you should become detached from the described route or need to make an emergency detour. The standard map for walking in the area is the OS Explorer map OL41 Forest of Bowland and Ribblesdale. In a double-sided format, this covers most of the walks, though refolding on top of the main ridge in a stiff breeze can be fun. In a few cases Explorer 287 West Pennine Moors is also required. Landranger maps (1:50,000) aren't really adequate for navigation on the fells but do provide context, though the Forest of Bowland falls awkwardly at the meeting of four sheets (97, 98, 102, 103).

Harvey maps are also excellent and are designed specifically for walkers and cyclists. They produce a Superwalker (1:25,000) map of the Forest of Bowland but it only covers the central area. (However it's backed with a 1:55,000 scale map of the entire area, which provides an unrivalled overview). It's also printed on waterproof paper, which can be a plus in these parts. Those walks which are fully covered at 1:25,000 on the Harvey Map are indicated 'Harvey'.

Reading the landscape

Navigation is not just about reading the map but also about reading the land. In particular, recognising a few common vegetation types gives valuable clues to the quality of footing that underlies them.

Bracken does not grow on waterlogged ground, making it a good indicator of firm footing. However, in high summer tall bracken can be hard to push through – and can also harbour sheep-ticks, which can transmit the very nasty Lyme Disease. In autumn and winter the rusty colour of old bracken is easily identified, and it then presents much less of an obstacle.

Heather: familiar to most people and covers swathes of the fells in brilliant purple during August. Heather does not like waterlogged ground, but its tough stems can be awkward to walk through, and can also sprawl over boulders, screening deep cracks and holes which can catch the unwary.

Bilberry: fresh green foliage often tinged with rusty hues. Likes similar habitats to heather and often grows intermingled, and can also conceal ankle-traps. Bilberries are excellent for snacking in autumn.

Rushes: rushes like damp ground and many walkers avoid them, but there's an old country saying: 'where rushes grow, a man can go', and it's nearly always true, as long as you are careful to stand firmly on the base of each clump. The ground between can be treacherous, but the rushes themselves often provide the best way across (or out of!) wet areas.

Blanket bog: a fascinating habitat, of which Bowland has some important examples, but no fun to walk across. Two tell-tale indicators are the vivid green of sphagnum moss (a superficially similar colour to young bracken) and the fluffy white heads of cotton grass.

Descriptions

I hope the route descriptions are clear and straightforward but there are just a couple of points worth noting. All route directions relate to direction of travel: I have not confused things by referring to the 'true left' bank of a stream or river. However, there are often subtle changes of direction when crossing stiles or passing from one field to another. In an effort to be as clear as possible about this, directions from gates or stiles relate to the alignment of that gate/stile, not to the previous direction of travel. For example, if the text says 'cross a stile and bear left', the 'left' should be understood as if you were standing with your back to the stile, irrespective of the direction you were travelling before you reached it.

Another point is that names of man-made features (farms, bridges, roads, etc.) are given in clear text if identification is obvious on first approach: e.g. walk down the street and turn left on Back Lane (assuming Back Lane has a street sign). However, if the name is only apparent later, or only from the map, it is given in brackets: e.g. walk down the field to a farm (Old Macdonald's Farm) and walk straight through the yard. I have not used this convention for the names of natural features, which as a rule do not have identifying signs and are part of the broader landscape context anyway.

Using this book
Units
I've used metric units throughout, with Imperial equivalents only in the chapter headings. I know many people still feel more comfortable with Imperial units, but I have a strong aversion to figures in brackets constantly cluttering up the pages. As a user I don't mind which system a book employs as long as it makes a firm decision to use one or the other. I've opted for metric in this book for several reasons, but the most important is that our maps (both OS and Harvey's) are essentially metric. Contour intervals are generally 10m on the OS Explorer maps, (although this is reduced to 0 5m on predominantly lowland maps such as Explorer 287), 10m on OS Landranger and 15m on the Harvey Superwalker. On all these maps the grid squares are 1km. Metric distances are therefore much easier to relate to map information.

If you still hanker after Imperial units, distances in metres are easily converted to yards: just add ten per cent and you'll be close enough.

Wildlife
Birds
For company on the fells, there are the ubiquitous grouse. The wilder the location, the better the chances of spotting the magnificent hen harrier (emblem of the AONB). The female is brown and may easily be mistaken for a buzzard, but has a distinctive white rump. The smaller male is silvery with black wingtips and unlikely to be mistaken for anything else. Buzzards are widespread in the valleys and on the lower slopes. Other raptors that may be seen include the peregrine and merlin, and the red kite has begun to move into the region.

Both in the rougher pastures and on the moors, ground-nesting birds are abundant and it's vital to take care where you step in spring and early summer. More and more of the farmland is once again being managed sympathetically to sustain populations of species like the beautiful lapwing. However, despite the claims of the hen harrier, no bird is more emblematic of Bowland than the curlew; it may be seen and heard from valley to fell top and its bubbling call (a territorial signal) is utterly evocative of the open spaces.

Mammals
While deer (especially roe deer), foxes and badgers are all found in Bowland, the largest

mammal that's regularly seen on these walks and rides is the brown hare, perhaps not because it's more abundant but because its preference for open habitats makes it conspicuous, especially when it bursts abruptly from cover, maybe only a few metres away, and streaks off across the ground. Another mammal that I seem to see reasonably frequently in Bowland is the stoat: on one of the mountain bike routes I was once preparing to take an action photo when a stoat passed so close to me that I couldn't focus on it with my telephoto lens (which means it was less than 1.8m away!).

It's an under-appreciated fact that wildlife encounters can be more frequent on a bike than on foot. This may be due to the greater speed and silence of the bike, and it's possible that many animals are slower to recognise a cyclist as a potentially dangerous biped. Whatever the reasons, my experience certainly bears out the point. Solo travellers will undoubtedly see more than those who walk/ride in a group.

There's lots more information about typical wildlife and habitats on the AONB website – www.forestofbowland.com.

Access

Before the Countryside and Rights of Way Act 2000 (CROW), which came fully into force in 2005, access to much of upland Bowland was severely restricted; it was often cited as one of the worst access black spots in the country. Since the 'Right to Roam' was introduced, all that has changed, and we can now walk freely across the moors. However, the dire predictions of some landowners and other interest about hordes of ramblers tramping (or should that be 'trampling') willy-nilly across the fragile moorland habitat have largely been disproved. As short sections of a few of the walks demonstrate, walking these fells away from established paths can be a tough proposition. Our routes mostly use existing rights of way and other paths and tracks, especially the shooters' tracks.

On cultivated land and in woodland the access situation is much as before and in general access is limited to designated rights of way. Cyclists are further restricted as they cannot legally ride on footpaths. For more on mountain bike access see the intro to that section.

There are some restrictions on open access land, including closure of some areas on certain days, usually during the grouse shooting season. Such closures are limited to a maximum of 28 days for any given parcel of land, and will not include Bank Holidays, Saturdays between 1st June and 11th August or Sundays between 1st June and 30th September. Further restrictions may occasionally be posted for conservation reasons and will be well signed in the vicinity.

Dogs

The other main restriction on access land is that much of it (basically areas used for rearing of grouse) is not open to dogs, other than guide dogs. Outside these areas, dogs should be kept on a lead not more than 2m in length during the nesting season (March–July) to protect ground-nesting birds. This restriction applies at any time near livestock. No such formal

restriction applies on footpaths or bridleways but it is of course sensible to keep dogs on lead whenever livestock is nearby. Even the best-trained dog may find it hard to resist the urge to chase when a hare rises suddenly, and at hare-chasing speeds those sheep 'over there' may suddenly be a lot closer.

An extending lead will allow the dog much greater freedom, and seems a good compromise most of the time, but please take care on routes shared with cyclists. The hard-to-see extending lead is often a greater menace to both dog and bike than when the dog is free.

It does sometimes happen that the tables are turned: cows, in particular, can occasionally decide to chase dogs. If this should happen most experts recommend letting go of the lead, as both dog and human are then better able to take care of themselves.

Public transport

Public transport in the area is not bad but not great either. More than half of the circular walks can be accessed by bus but I have not been slavish about it and certainly have not excluded good walks because they are remote from usable bus services. For those who have the choice these walks are pretty certain to be accessed by car, but for those who are dependent on public transport I have tried to indicate options that may be available, though they may entail walking (or maybe hitching) significant extra distances.

Using public transport where practical has many advantages, from salving your Green conscience to allowing everyone to enjoy a post-hike pint or two. Perhaps best of all, it frees the walker from the need to return to the same place you started from, and this opens up a

Above: Watching the paragliders from the slopes of Parlick. Right: Early stages of the climb from High Salter (north to south route M4)

whole new range of possibilities. The linear walks can be linked up to form a fine tour (five or six days) of the area. With one debatable exception, they can also all be readily enjoyed as one-day walks in their own right.

Unlike enlightened countries like Switzerland, buses in Britain do not generally carry bikes and therefore options for accessing the rides by public transport are much more limited. However, several of the road bike rides do start from rail stations. The mountain bike rides are generally more remote from rail services though M3 and M1 are reasonably accessible from Wennington.

Long distance routes

A number of longer distance walking routes pass through the region, including the Ribble Way, Pendle Way and Wyre Way. This last-named has the most substantial presence in Bowland, with about a third of its 72km in the AONB, including a loop to link the Tarnbrook and Marshaw branches of the Wyre. Walks C2 and C3 partly coincide with the Wyre Way. L1 is essentially the same as the first half of the Lune Valley Ramble.

There is also the Journey Through the Centre of the Kingdom, a 75km route (almost as long as its name!) starting in Clitheroe and looping through Dunsop Bridge, allegedly the geographical centre of Great Britain.

All the above are for walkers only; for cyclists (and horse riders) there is the North Lancashire Bridleway. Currently only half a circle, this 47km route runs from Chipping to Dunsop Bridge (see Ride M2), then on to Slaidburn (not such great trails for biking), over Salter Fell to Roeburndale (M4) and then by Caton Moor (M1) to Caton and the Lune Valley. In effect all the good bits are included in our routes anyway. However, the story may not end there as the intention is ultimately to make it a complete loop. As and when this comes to fruition (especially if the route goes where I think it will) this will be a really exciting development.

Finally, for road bike riders there's the Lancashire Cycleway. This is often described as looking like a squashed figure 8, its two loops meeting at Whalley in the Ribble valley. Having

diplomatically hedged my bets in the official guidebook to the route, let me now come clean and say that the Northern loop is undoubtedly finer – and a lot of it is in the Bowland AONB, including the crossing of Cross o'Greet. The full loop, by my bike computer, is 205.8 kilometres or 127.8 miles, and also takes in the lowlands of the Fylde and the delights of the Arnside and Silverdale AONB.

Walk C1 Clougha Pike

A grand little walk, but not to be underestimated

Distance: 8.2km (5.1 miles)
Ascent: 382m (1,255ft)
Minimum Time: 2½ hours, but it's worth taking a lot longer.
Underfoot: Moorland walking with some very rough paths. Boggy sections are short but make their presence felt.
Public transport: Nothing of practical value.
Parking: Access Area car park at Birk Bank.
Public toilets: Nothing nearby.
Dogs: Now permitted (restriction signs relate to access agreements predating CRoW).
Refreshments: No refreshments en route. For après-hike the nearest possibilities are in Caton, the Fleece Inn near Dolphinholme, or there's a great range in Lancaster.
Maps: OL41, Harvey
Start: SD 526 604

I used to live on the other side of the Quernmore valley; I'd see Clougha every day and climbed

Setting out on a frosty day

it often (and I still can see it from the bedroom window in Garstang). I've certainly made over 100 ascents, probably nearer 200, and I still look forward to coming back for the next. With that experience behind me I feel fairly confident in saying that this is the best route up and down. In fact, if there's a better short walk in Lancashire I don't know how I've missed it. Short it may be, at least in map distance, but it's often rough and deserves respect. On a clear day the views are magnificent but I've done it in thick mist and still enjoyed it. Near or far, there's always something to see.

The Walk

1. Follow the track rising from the car park, then fork left. It becomes a green path running generally level, with one wet patch, to a small aqueduct (Ottergear Bridge). Cross the bridge and bear left on a level track, which contours around the hill. Keep right at the next junction. The track rises then drops into a narrow valley, crosses a stile and climbs steeply again. As the track eases and swings right, break off left on a narrow, rough path, running almost level above a steeper slope. After 500m, it angles back down into the valley.

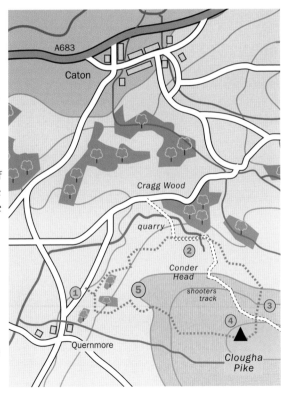

This little valley is the first of several odd channels on the flank of Clougha Pike, of which Windy Clough is the most striking; we'll see it on the descent. The channels were formed at the end of the last Ice Age, when the edge of the ice-sheet lay on or behind the ridge. Torrents of meltwater, some of them probably running under pressure beneath the ice underneath it, created the chaotic network of channels

2. Follow the base of the steep slope and cross a small stream. About 30m further on a green track climbs to the right. Wind up steeply to the near-level moor. The path follows a slight groove,

trending left towards a wall, but straightens out before reaching it. The line is a bit vague across a level boggy area, but becomes much clearer as the ground starts to rise again. A clear groove develops; the path sometimes follows this, sometimes runs alongside, as it climbs steadily past old shooting butts. The groove is continuous and clear until it meets a shooters' 4x4 track. (This is actually the same track we were on at the last stile, and we could have followed it all the way, but it's much less interesting).

3. Cross the shooters' track and follow a narrow grassy path past occasional decaying marker stakes. Bear right up a slight rise and join a wider path on a broad ridge. Go right, cross a fence and continue gently down to the summit trig point. Yes, that's right, go down to the summit. (It makes perfect sense from the Quernmore valley).

Despite its lack of true summit stature, the top of Clougha is one of the finest viewpoints in Bowland. On a decent day the Clwydian Hills in Wales are easily seen beyond the Lancashire lowlands. The higher, but more distant, peaks of Snowdonia (the Carneddau, principally) are less frequently sighted, but the Isle of Man is often spotted floating beyond the shipyard

Above: Climbing the grooved path with Morecambe Bay behind. Opposite page: the summit of Clougha Pike.

cranes of Barrow. However, nothing can really compete with the melodrama of the Lakeland skyline. High ground sweeps on east, over the Howgill Fells and into Yorkshire, where Whernside, Ingleborough and Pen-y-Ghent all stand out.

4. Turn right at the trig column, following a clear path. The steep face of Clougha, littered with boulders and a few small crags, is below on the left. A fence converges from the right, eventually meeting a wall, in which a gap has recently appeared. I hope it wasn't deliberately made by walkers just to avoid the brief scramble down around the end of the wall. Continue down a rough path just left of the wall for about 250m to a level place above scattered boulders (about 50m before a bend in the wall). Go down left, through a gap flanked by wrinkled rocks, then across open and sometimes boggy slopes to a gate by the corner of another wall.

Descend straight ahead until the ground steepens. The path swings right and wanders down in the direction of Windy Clough. Drop down to a stile at a junction of walls

5. Cross and go left down a grooved path to an area of young trees. Fork left, moving closer to the stream; there are several alternative routes here but this is the driest and becoming the most used.

The various routes soon rejoin and the path descends through gorse then follows duckboards along the edge of a bog. Go up to a track, turn right, then keep left over a slight rise and descend back to the car park.

Walk C2 Tarnbrook and Ward's Stone

From lush valley to the highest point of the true Bowland fells

Distance: 14.8km (9.2 miles)
Ascent: 517m (1,695ft)
Minimum Time: 3½ hours
Underfoot: Mostly good tracks but a short section of rough, trackless ground approaching the plateau and a rougher, often muddy path coming off it.
Public transport: Nothing of practical use to walkers.
Parking: Parking area alongside the Tarnbrook Wyre, beside the minor road, through the gate just east of Stoops Bridge on outskirts of Abbeystead.
Public toilets: None
Refreshments: No refreshments en route.
Dogs: Not allowed
Maps: OL41, Harvey
Start: SD 564 544

As the highest point of the Forest of Bowland, Ward's Stone is a natural target. It appears that most walkers give themselves a 'leg-up' by starting from Jubilee Tower, crossing the top of Grit Fell on the way. This is a decent walk but rather one-dimensional, especially as it's out and back by the same route. The round suggested here is only a couple of kilometres longer – though it involves significantly more ascent – but it's a much richer and more rounded route. A gradual approach gives time to survey the objective; a good track makes light of the main

ascent and then there's a short but interesting pathless section onto the bare plateau. A fine swinging descent and a pleasant warm-down through the valley complete a thoroughly satisfying outing – and that's without even mentioning the views.

The Walk

1. Just south of the parking area, on the opposite side of the road, is the start of a track beside a wall, with a Wyre Way (WW) sign. Follow this; go through a gate and straight ahead, joining a fence alongside pheasant pens. Cross a footbridge over the Marshaw Wyre and bear slightly left to climb a bank. Continue roughly parallel to the river below, looking for a low stone WW marker, then bear left and go down left to another footbridge.

Cross and bear left along the boundary wall around the formal gardens of Abbeystead House. Climb steeply through trees then slant up right before a small stream to emerge into a level field. Follow its left edge then bear right to two stiles at the crossing of a surfaced track. Continue straight ahead, with a field edge just on the right, then turn right through a muddy gateway or over a stile alongside. Continue along a bank between ditches, then keep straight ahead to a stile onto a road.

2. Go straight ahead into a farm track (Top of Emmetts). Just before the farm go right over a stile and follow the field edge into the corner. Cross the stile, follow the fence line a short way then cross two stiles and a plank bridge. Bear left, aiming towards a barn (only the roof is visible at first). Cross another stile and pass right of the barn, then follow the field edge down. Cross the end of a track and continue straight ahead over several stiles, bearing slightly right to a gateway and the start of a rough track overlooking the river (the Tarnbrook Wyre).

Follow the track down and bear left to a bridge. Cross and go up between walls to a lane in the hamlet of Tarnbrook. Go right a few

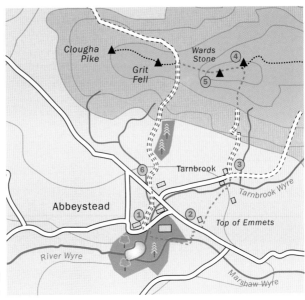

Opposite page: Crossing pastures early in the walk: Hawthornthwaite Fell behind.

metres then turn left on a track, going through a gate groaning under the weight of restriction signs.

3. Follow the track steadily up the hill, with switchbacks at the steepest part. Pass a rough path going off right (this gives access to Thorn Crag) and then a branch track to left. (If mist has descended, this track can be followed, eventually meeting the descent route at a T-junction). In clear weather, or if you fancy a bit of an adventure, keep straight on up until the track ends at a small parking area. From the top left corner a small path continues, promisingly at first, but then wandering off to the right. Leave it where it dips to cross a beck.

The route from here is pathless and requires improvisation, but the surroundings are interesting and in their own moody way quite beautiful, following the stream course and then threading across a heathery plateau stippled with small pools (many of which disappear in dry weather). The basic heading is due north but you'll need to weave around it a bit to keep a good footing. Gradually the heather gives way to grass and sedge before you reach the plateau with its expanses of bare ground and curious inselbergs of peat. With luck or good navigation you'll arrive near the eastern top, whose trig point is at 561m.

4. Follow an indistinct path west across

Top: The pathless heathery plateau between shooters' track and summit ridge.
Above: On the western top of Ward's Stone

the plateau to reach the western top, a metre lower but arguably more attractive with its jumbled outcrops. The ground falls away to west and north, giving fine views in these directions, to the Lune Estuary, Morecambe Bay and the Lakeland fells.

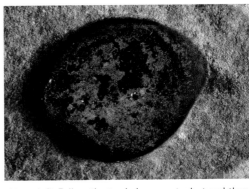

5. Descend west on a clearer path, initially rocky and then levelling out and tangling with some muddy patches. Eventually meet another shooters' track and turn left. Follow the track down past a hut and then a parking area by a junction (this is where the mist-safe option rejoins).

Continue straight ahead down the track, into fields and past a dark plantation, before it swings down to pass a handsome house (Higher Lee). Follow the track away from this, through a yard and out to a road. Turn left down the road for approx 400m to an entrance on the right.

6. Cross a stile beside a gate and follow the track ahead; this is used, in the other direction, by Walk C3. Follow the track, which later runs beside the river (Tarnbrook Wyre), for a little over 1km to the outskirts of Abbeystead. Turn left along the road to cross Stoops Bridge then immediately right to the parking area.

Top: Pool in rock near the west top. Above: On the descent to Higher Lee.

Walk C3 Wyresdale

The shortest proper walk in this book – but good things come in small packages

Distance: 6.4km (4 miles)
Ascent: 139m (455ft)
Minimum time: 2¼ hours
Underfoot: Mostly good paths and tracks, route sometimes vague across fields.
Public transport: Nothing of real use.
Parking: Parking places near Christ Church (The Shepherds' Church), Over Wyresdale. There are services most Sundays at 11am and parking can be more difficult at these times.
Public toilets: None
Refreshments: No refreshments en route; the Fleece Inn is just down the valley for that post-hike pint.
Maps: OL41
Start: SD 552 543

With its woods, waters and green pastures surrounded by high bald fells, Wyresdale is quintessential Bowland; who would dispute that it's one of the finest valleys in the region? This short walk is an excellent way to sample its delights. If that wasn't appealing enough, it starts from the most beautifully situated church in Lancashire.

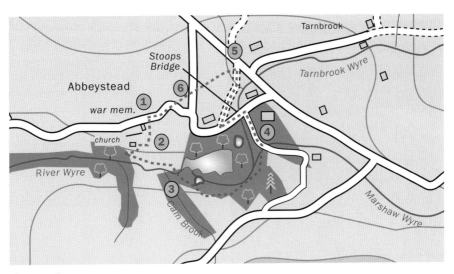

The Walk

1. Walk down the church entrance track and round to the main door, which faces the valley. Alternatively, especially if parked further west, cross a stile by a footpath sign about 100m west of the Church entrance. Descend the field then cross the stream and over two stiles into the churchyard and walk round to the main door.

From the church door go straight ahead to a metal gate, where you find the first of a series of beautiful hand-carved marker stones (all different, too) which you'll encounter along this route. Head straight down the field to a foot-bridge and then over two stiles. Climb the bank above the second to another marker stone and follow its direction across a large field towards Lentworth House. Head straight towards the first house, go through a kissing gate just before it and turn left on a track.

2. Keep straight ahead into the farmyard and then go through the left-hand of two gates, over a stile and down the fence to another stile. Bear right, descending with a wood on your left, to cross a track to another stile. Descend through the wood (slippery stone steps) and then down the field to a footbridge over the Wyre. Do not cross but turn left, keeping to the slightly higher level in the two-tier

Opposite page: The Shepherds' Church, Abbeystead. Above: Marker stone before Lentworth House.

fields ahead, passing a couple of waymarked posts. Join a track which runs straight ahead, leading to waterworks buildings.

Look for the memorial stone on the left as you arrive at the waterworks, commemorating a disaster in 1984. Thirty-six villagers from St Michael's-on-Wyre, in the lowlands below Garstang, had been invited to see the recently constructed works to allay fears about flooding. Something, quite possibly a cigarette, ignited a build-up of methane. Eight people were killed instantly and eight more died later from injuries. The youngest victim was just eight years old.

3. Stay with the track until it bends left then go straight ahead to the corner of a wall. Go a few metres along the top edge to a gate and then down a steep path to a metal footbridge. Cross this and turn immediately left. The path runs alongside the outfall from the Abbeystead Reservoir and climbs to the level of the dam. Continue along the narrow but clear path beside the reservoir and then near the river until you eventually come up slightly to a road.

The reservoir was built in 1855 but is no longer in use. It's interesting to note here how much of it has silted up and become at least semi-solid ground. Studies by Lancaster University's Environmental Science department suggest that less than 30 per cent of the original area remains as open water while the water volume is down to less than 6 per cent.

4. Turn left and cross a bridge. The water below is the Marshaw branch of the Wyre; the confluence with the Tarnbrook Wyre is only about 100m downstream but out of sight from the path. Incidentally, the naming of two branches of a river like this (Tarnbrook Wyre and Marshaw Wyre) is quite rare.

Turn left at a T-junction, cross a bridge (Stoops Bridge) and walk to the first house of Abbeystead village. Opposite the first house, turn right over a stile then join a track which runs parallel to the river (Tarnbrook Wyre). Follow this track, eventually leaving the river, for about 1km. Ignore a sign and footbridge off to the right and continue to the end where a stile by a gate leads to a road.

The core of the village, just beyond the next rise, is really just a hamlet of half a dozen estate houses, but it is the nucleus for a substantial rural population. There's a new, environmentally friendly village hall, and a primary school (Cawthorne's Endowed School) with around 30 pupils. The village is believed to stand on the site of a short-lived 12th-century Cistercian abbey, but there are no visible remains.

5. Turn left immediately over another stile and go straight up the rise to find a footbridge near the top – looking rather oversize for the tiny stream it crosses. Bear slightly right from the bridge and walk through the next rough pasture, keeping to the top of a steep bank that divides it, to find another stile in a wire fence. From this go straight ahead along the left edge of two fields. Pass a small pool and descend into a dip just beyond where there's a stile under a thorn tree. Cross then continue in the same direction, picking up a track, which runs virtually straight, to a road.

6. Go straight across to a stile. In the absence of a trodden path across this field, aim directly for the short stretch of road that can be seen at the far side (right of the church tower). Join the road at a stile and follow it back to the church.

Opposite page: Crossing the footbridge below Abbeystead Reservoir.
Above: Bluebells in the woods near Stoops Bridge.

Walk C4 Brennand Great Hill and Wolfhole Crag

A terrific trek to Bowland's loneliest summit

Distance: 14.3km (8.9 miles)
Ascent: 485m (1,591ft)
Minimum time: 4½ hours
Underfoot: Most of the distance is on good tracks but it's the rougher sections that stick in the mind. Navigation can be tricky on Brennand Great Hill in bad weather.
Public transport: None.
Parking: riverside opposite Tower Lodge
Public toilets: None.
Refreshments: None.
Dogs: Not allowed.
Maps: OL41, Harvey
Start: Tower Lodge, Trough of Bowland road SD 604 538

A certain bleak magnificence is the keynote of this often lonely walk, yet there is considerable variety, from the pretty and popular pine-shaded Marshaw Wyre to the buttercup-strewn pastures of the Tarnbrook valley. Wolfhole Crag is probably the furthest of the Bowland tops from a public road, but good tracks and paths mean it isn't the hardest to reach. Still, the

sense of isolation is strong and the views are superb. If wild moorland expanses appeal, then Wolfhole Crag is absolutely not to be missed.

When done in the direction described almost all the ascent is on good tracks and this has to be the easier way to do the walk. The trackless expanses below Brennand Great Hill are then taken in descent, which also has to be easier. However, if bad weather appears likely later in the day, taking the route in reverse gets the more exposed sections out of the way sooner and from Brennand Great Hill onwards navigation is pretty foolproof.

The Walk

1. Walk up the track beside Tower Lodge for about 400m to a metal gate. A short distance above this is a finger-post. One arm points half-left (to Gilberton) – but go straight ahead to cross a stream before following the indicated direction. Thread through rushes and then climb a steeper slope covered in thistles to find a stile in a stone wall. From this go diagonally to a wooden stile in a fence on the ridge and then follow a faint path to a gate and stile. Cross, and descend near the wall, passing a narrow wood (Harry Wood). Continue along a fence and then through the left-hand of two gates slightly above two barns. Enter the enclosure between the barns and bear left along a track.

2. Just before reaching a farm (Gilberton) go right to cross a wooden footbridge. Join the farm track, crossing a cattle grid. Continue to another cattle grid and a junction just beyond. Go right and start to climb, winding up a steeper section then continuing more gradually again.

Several rashes of rocks decorate the steeper slope below the skyline. The highest and furthest left is Thorn Crag. It may look like no more than a collection of large boulders but the scale is deceptive and there

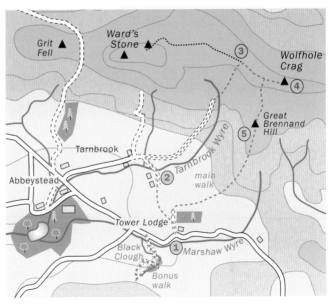

Opposite page: At the summit of Wolfhole Crag, looking south.

are some significant and hard rock-climbs here, notably The Last Temptation, which weighs in at a worrying E6 6b. I was lucky enough to be there to photograph the renowned climber Dave Pegg on the first ascent.

Keep plugging up the track, passing another track which joins in from the left just below the broken rocks of Long Crag. Just beyond this the track levels out and then forks. Either branch will work, but the right-hand route is prettier, threading between crags and cascades – and it avoids an unnecessary up and down. The path crosses the stream then swings left to rejoin the main track. The track continues across an undulating plateau, eventually reaching the ridge fence where the Three Peaks of Yorkshire suddenly appear.

3. Don't cross the fence but turn right parallel to it, following a vague vehicle track (probably a gamekeeper's quad-bike). Soon enough this peters out, near where the fence straddles an area of bare peat. Continue close to the fence on a narrow path: the going is surprisingly easy. Arrive at two kissing gates and a rash of signs; continue straight ahead, now following a wall. A slight rise soon leads to the boulder-strewn west top of Wolfhole Crag. Continue through a slight dip to the trig point on the east top, officially two metres higher and the high point of the walk.

It's worth continuing 100m or so further east to the largest of the boulders, which are large enough to have a couple of described routes in early editions of the British Mountaineering Council's Lancashire rock climbing guide, though they don't even rate a mention in the current volume.

4. Retrace your steps to the kissing gate, go through, and then turn left alongside the fence (signed for Miller's House). The path here is pretty faint, but don't knock it – it's all we've got. Although we're generally descending now, the going is the toughest so far, with lots of little peaty dips. Old fence-posts often provide the firmest footing, but there are several wet patches to get round in the dip before the fence gives way to a wall and the ground gets firmer. The way rises past a large isolated boulder. This really deserves a name and the word 'elephant', carved in the rock, seems as good as any (is that 'rock' or 'rook' just to the right again?). It's easily climbed on its south side but there are several more challenging options, notably the groove and overhang just right of the carving. Continue along the wall to the high point, though it's hard to identify exactly where this lies.

5. Now comes the tricky bit. Getting off Brennand Great Hill is not really hard and certainly not dangerous, but the route is awfully vague and nearly impossible to describe. I've been up here at least eight times and never been the same way twice! There's no clear path, but lots of intermittent sheep-trods and faint quad-bike tracks, which seem to be in a state of flux. There are orange-topped marker posts but I find them completely unhelpful.

Where the descent steepens briefly, pause and survey the options. In bad visibility, unless you're confident with map and compass (or GPS), the safe (though longer) option is to follow the wall down, over the rocky rise of Miller's House (no houses to be seen). When you meet another wall turn right along it until you reach the stile. In clear weather it's easier to forget about this and simply head southwest (if you've no compass, aim for the highest part of the long ridge of Hawthornthwaite Fell). Make use of any vague path that seems to be heading in the right direction, but don't be led astray. The ground is often tussocky so a little care is needed; there are some wet patches but nothing that can't be easily avoided, or crossed by relying on rushes.

After a near-level stretch the slope steepens slightly and some more useful landmarks appear. You'll see the wall that runs along the ridge of White Moor, with a prominent lone pine tree above it. Look well to the right of this to pick out a tall ladder stile – this is what we're aiming for. The stile stands beside a (usually locked) gate and beyond it is a clear track.

6. All navigational worries are now behind us as the track runs straight down to Tower Lodge, rejoining the outward route about halfway down.

Opposite page: Boulders near the summit of Wolfhole Crag. Above: Ruined sheepfold high on Brennand Great Hill, looking towards Tarnbrook and Ward's Stone.

Bonus walk: Black Clough

Distance: 4.6km (2.9 miles)
Ascent: 245m (805ft)

Black Clough is a real hidden gem; the first time I discovered it I had no idea what was in store, and it's almost a shame I have to dilute the surprise for you. For anyone who's done the main walk above and has some energy left it's a delightful way to end the day, and it can also be easily snapped up whenever you're passing through the Marshaw valley.

The one drawback for those who've been on Wolfhole Crag is that the start is over 1km down the road from Tower Lodge (going towards Lancaster). It's tempting to drive down but there's no parking in the immediate vicinity. It might also be tempting to take a short-cut across country, but this is rough moor with no tracks but many awkward drainage ditches. The start is an obvious large metal gate about 150m east of the cattle grid at the start (west end) of the open pinewoods. Follow the obvious track across the river and continue for about 1.5km, swinging right, dipping to cross a beck and then rising slightly. Fork left into a parking area with a stone shooters' hut just beyond. Walk past the hut and into the wooded clough. Explore as far as you wish. To penetrate all the way requires a little mild scrambling and/or a tolerance of wet feet, but reveals some delightful little cascades and brings the fullest sense of isolation. One can feel just as far from the workaday world here as on the top of Wolfhole Crag. Tread carefully to minimise disturbance to the delicate vegetation, or I'll wish I'd never mentioned Black Clough.

You may retrace your steps when you feel you can go no further, or you may reach a point where you emerge above the trees into a more open upper valley where bog-myrtle flourishes. At this point turn right and go straight up the slope. It will be a struggle through dense vegetation but

it's only about 100m to a parking circle at the terminus of the shooters' track.

Feel free to explore further but I strongly recommend returning to the bog-myrtle basin and then making for the shooters' track, as progress in any other direction is likely to prove extremely slow and frustrating (though it might make you appreciate how easy Brennand Great Hill really is!)

Above: Waterfall in Black Clough. Opposite page: Plenty of waymarks on the first stretch of C5

Walk C5 Grizedale Head

Bowland in the rough – not for the faint-hearted

Distance: 12.4km (7.7 miles)
Ascent: 450m (1,475ft)
Minimum time: 4¼ hours
Underfoot: Some rough and pathless stretches, but the fields early on are the boggiest part.
Public transport: Nothing nearby but can be linked with Scorton via Walk C6 (see Bonus Walk at the end of this chapter).
Parking: Small parking area at Grizedale Bridge, or anywhere suitable on verges to the north.
Public toilets: None
Refreshments: No refreshments en route.
Dogs: No
Maps: OL41, Harvey
Start: SD 536 491

A long, almost level ridge bounds Wyresdale on the south; from a distance it looks as if it should give miles of easy walking, but like several other Bowland tops, appearances are deceptive. True, there's some bare ground and stretches of well-defined path around the highest point, Hawthornthwaite Fell Top (479m) but getting there is not a straightforward business. The nicest route would be via Black Clough (see previous section) but above this is some of the most rampant heather in all of Bowland. The most obvious route is by the steep shooters' track which starts near Well Brook Farm at 582 535; when this runs out look for a

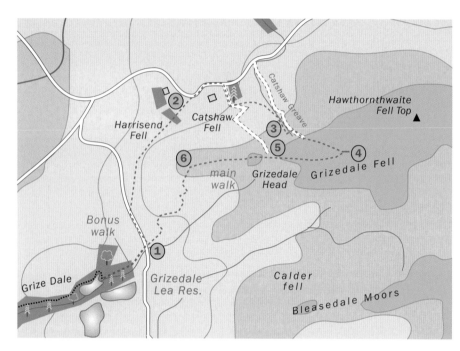

faint path heading half-right; follow this until it reaches the bare upper slopes. Return the same way. The route described here does not reach the highest point but concentrates on the western end of the ridge, which has terrific views over Wyresdale and Morecambe Bay. The first half is thoroughly enjoyable and there's a good finish, especially lovely when the sun's sinking over Morecambe Bay. However, in between there can be some tough going – though generally down-hill – over luxuriant heather and bilberry. Conditions vary according to which bits have been cut or burned most recently. At least the fence along the ridge means you shouldn't get lost.

The Walk

1. Follow the road uphill and away from the bridge, with the high heathery slope on your right and widening views on the left. As the road begins to descend, take a signed footpath on the right. It's narrow but clear enough, curving round the hillside and keeping roughly level. Follow it to signs and a gate where you leave access land. The route (there's no obvious path) now follows field edges, sticking roughly to a contour. The general rule is to keep the field boundary just to your left, but there's a bit of a jiggle going round the lower end of a narrow belt of new tree planting, and again through a dip with a stream. Keep ploughing through, always on the same general heading, to a stile leading onto a road.

Above: Catshaw Greave

2. Turn right and follow the road for about a kilometre. With less need to watch where you're stepping, it's a good chance to enjoy the fine scene of Wyresdale, looking across to Ward's Stone and Brennand Hill (Walks C2 and C4).

Cross a cattle-grid and turn right immediately up a track beside a conifer plantation. Follow the tracks as it bends left but leave it where it bends sharply back right. Head to an obvious post; just beyond is a rush-filled groove which could be an old track. You could follow this but it loses some of the height you've just gained, and isn't really any easier, so cross it instead. Now follow vague sheep tracks through the dense heather.

There are multiple possibilities but the idea is to follow as level a line as possible. As the slope curves round another surfaced track appears. Head for a small parking area, where a footbridge takes you across the stream.

3. Follow the track, climbing steeply for a way, up the fine valley of Catshaw Greave. Above the steepest climb, the map reveals that the fellside opposite rejoices in the name of Pig's Face, though I couldn't see the resemblance.

Above: Grizedale Head

The track ends at another small parking area. A narrow, rough path heads up right to a marker post but soon fades. The ground here changes from year to year as strips of heather are cut or burned and the easiest plan is to improvise a route linking these cleared strips. Stay on the open slopes, keeping roughly parallel to the upper reaches of Catshaw Greave. Keep an eye out ahead for a couple of gates, where two fences meet on Greave Clough Head.

4. Go through the left of the two gates and turn right to go through the second gate. Keep the fence on your right, though you'll need to deviate more than a few times to negotiate channels in the peat. After about a kilometre of gradual descent, the fence bears right. You might want to cross to the other side to take advantage of cleared ground, but these strips aren't necessarily permanent. There's a slight rise onto Grizedale Head, and then another gate in the fence.

5. If you crossed to its right side earlier, cross back to the left now and continue, soon picking up something more like a permanent path. Follow this for almost 2km, always near the fence, to a cairn on a small rise. Just beyond is a gate. Go through and descend straight down the slope, heading for a large cairn about 400m away. Cross another fence – hidden from the gate. Nearby is an old boundary stone – Hayshaw Fell 1846. The big cairn has a terrific view over the lowlands and out to Morecambe Bay.

6. Turn left and follow sheep-tracks or strips of cleared ground. Avoid descending left into Breast Moss Hole. A vague ridge develops, leading to a slight rise with another cairn. Weather permitting, Grizedale Lea and Barnacre reservoirs are a good landmark ahead. A fair path now leads down the hill and back to Grizedale Bridge.

Bonus walk: Grizedale Lea 4km

While you're at Grizedale Bridge, it's well worth taking a walk down the path which runs west from the parking area, near a wall. Go through a sheepfold then turn left on a permitted path. Cross a stream and continue into woodland. The clear path now runs for almost a kilometre through a delightful hidden valley, with some sections of duckboards to protect fragile ground. At the end the path emerges onto a broader track alongside the head of Grizedale Reservoir. Continue as far as you wish and then retrace.

Link to Scorton

Better still, if you can conjure up a decent rural bus service, or get someone to drop you off at Grizedale Bridge, turn this into a linear walk to Scorton. When the track meets another by the head of the reservoir, turn left. After 150m there's a stile on the right which gives the opportunity to go over Nicky Nook (first half of Walk C6, in reverse). It's equally enjoyable and even easier (99 per cent downhill) to stick with the waterside track and follow C6 as described all the way into Scorton.

Walk C6 Nicky Nook and Grize Dale

A local favourite, and for very good reasons

Distance: 7.3km (4.5 miles)
Ascent: 285m (935ft)
Minimum time: 2¼ hours
Underfoot: Mostly well-drained paths on the fell, good tracks in the valley, a few fields and quiet lanes.
Public transport: Garstang Super 8 Service 8S (Monday–Saturday, 3 times daily) links Scorton with Garstang and its regular services to/from Lancaster, Preston and Blackpool. There's also an easy walking link (about 1km) direct from the A6 (use the stops near Weavers caravan park).
Parking: On the road just south of village centre. Cars could also be parked on Snow Hill Lane just above the motorway bridge, saving the first climb out of Scorton.
Public toilets: Pay toilets by the road just south of the village centre.
Refreshments: The Barn and the Priory in Scorton
Maps: OL41
Start: SD 503 487

The solitude of the Bowland Fells is more elusive on Nicky Nook. In dozens of visits I don't think I've ever had the hill entirely to myself. You're also – especially with a westerly wind – likely to be reminded that this is very much a western outlier of the fells and its top is less than 2km from the M6. But the fact that it's a western outlier, poised between fell and plain,

also means that it is one of the best viewpoints in Bowland. It certainly delivers its view for a lot less effort than most of the fells. Nicky Nook is a neat little hill with good paths, most of which are well-drained and easy to follow.

You can stomp up and down from the nearest road in half an hour, but it's much more satisfying to combine Nicky Nook with the fine valley of Grize Dale; starting and finishing in the compact but well-serviced village of Scorton makes it an even more complete excursion.

The Walk

1. Walk up the steep road, Snow Hill Lane, just right of the Priory hotel/restaurant. Pass the Catholic church, cross over the M6 and follow the road round left as it levels out. Leave houses behind and come to a sort of crossroads, though only the right-most route is a public road. Follow this down to cross a stream then steeply up to a T-junction.

2. Go straight ahead over a stile onto the fellside and climb an obvious steep path through gorse and bracken. Skirt the left side of a small reservoir, follow the wall on the left and continue to a gap at the left end of another wall. Bear right on a green track, which crosses a clearer track and climbs gradually onto the ridge, trending left to the trig point.

3. Continue straight ahead (the left fork of the path), descending slightly to a stile in a wall. Continue past a curious stone pillar and then descend more steeply, joining a stony track bearing left. Just before this meets a wider track, go right to a kissing gate and then turn right on the wide track. Follow this down through a couple of gates to level out alongside Grizedale Reservoir. Just before the lake a sign on the left marks the start of the permissive path up Grizedale Lea, a charming detour (see walk 5 Bonus). Continue down the main track with the water on your left. Pass the dam and descend

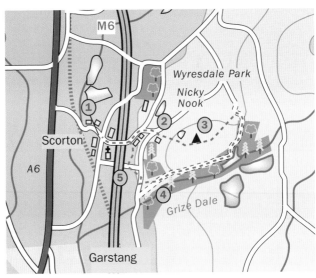

Opposite: On the ridge of Nicky Nook. with Clougha, Grit Fell and Ward's Stone on the horizon.

steeply for a stretch, then continue down the level valley until you reach another gate across the track.

4. There's a footbridge across the beck, but turn right, away from it, and up the track to a road (Higher Lane). Continue straight ahead, uphill then, as the lane levels out, turn left at a footpath sign. Go down the field edge until below the farm buildings on the left but still well above a house with a wind turbine then bear right to a gate, which, on arrival, is actually a stile. Continue towards a small blockhouse style building and cross a stile into the enclosure around it. Cross another stile by the corner of the building into a drive and follow it out to a lane (Tithe Barn Lane).

5. Turn left down the lane, which swings right at a cluster of houses and runs more level. Pass one footpath sign on the right then take the next, just as the road starts to bend left and drop down to the motorway. Cross a field into woodland and follow the path into an unexpected steep-sided, shady little valley. Cross the stream and rise the other side before emerging into the open. Keep to the same heading then bear left on a short track out to a road; this is Snow Hill Lane again. Turn left back down into Scorton.

Above: Descending into Scorton. Opposite: Looking across Bleasdale to Parlick early in the morning.

Walk C7 Bleasdale

No summits, but who needs them?

Distance: 11.5 km (7.1 miles)
Ascent: 430m (1,410ft)
Minimum time: 3¼ hours
Underfoot: Tarmac (virtually traffic-free) estate roads, fields, moorland tracks.
Public transport: Nothing actually to the start, but Garstang Super 8 Service 8C runs to Calder Vale (Monday–Saturday, three times daily). The link from Calder Vale to Delph Lane – approx 1.5km – reverses part of Walk L5.
Parking: Small car park at an old quarry on Delph Lane.
Public toilets: None.
Refreshments: No refreshments en route; the tea room at Cobble Hey Farm is a short drive away or can be reached by a detour at the end of the walk.
Maps: OL41, Harvey
Start: SD 546 456

Bleasdale is one of those bits of landscape that's so perfect it seems like a work of art. The image of a bowl is unavoidable; everyone uses it. True, it's a bowl that's tipped a bit to one side, with a wobbly rim, but it's still a bowl. You feel enfolded by the hills. The private estate roads offer lots of easy walking through the valley, but this route breaks out onto the higher northern rim and then coasts along just below the skyline before gliding back down. One wet field and one short steep climb are a very small price to pay.

The Walk

1. Walk up the lane, soon levelling out, for 200m to a permissive access sign on the right. Follow the short track through the trees then turn right down the edge of the field. Follow the waymarked route going left at the bottom of the slope, then right down the far side of another plantation and along the field edge to near a farm (High Moor). Turn left to another

St Eadmer's Church

Its dedication is thought to be unique, and in fact Eadmer – a historian and theologian who lived around 1060–1124 – was never officially canonised, so isn't strictly a saint at all. The first records of a chapel here are from the late 16th century but the present church mostly dates to the 1830s.

Bleasdale Circle

Bleasdale Circle is thought to date to the Bronze Age. Its complex and enigmatic structure was based on two circles around a single grave. The original timber posts have been replaced by prosaic concrete stubs, and it's hard to get a sense of the whole circle or its alignment as the site is surrounded and overshadowed by trees. Finds from the site can now be seen at the splendid Harris Museum in Preston.

Above: Looking across Bleasdale towards Beacon Fell.

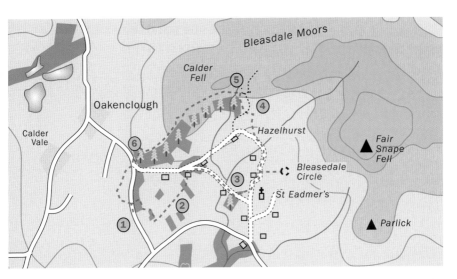

farm (Broadgate). Keep right of the buildings to a kissing gate and turn right along a track. At its end continue across a field to a track through Broadgate Wood.

The fields either side of Delph Lane are now all managed to encourage wildlife, and support significant breeding populations of lapwing, snipe and other waders. For more information about this, and access to a couple of hides, visit Cobble Hey Farm.

2. Leaving the wood, bear left up a field (often wet) to the far corner. Go through a kissing gate and along a fence, overlooked by Bleasdale Tower. Keep straight ahead to reach a tarmac road and go right. (Several estate cottages and farm buildings line a branch road on the left). Keep straight ahead again at the next fork and soon pass another farm (Brooks). Look out for the little packhorse bridge to the left of the road where you cross the River Brock. Soon a rougher track bears off left, under some tall pines.

3. Take this track and keep straight ahead across a field, then skirt below a house to meet another road just below the little church of St Eadmer. Turn left up the road and follow it past Vicarage Farm. Here a sign indicates a path off to the right to Bleasdale Circle, which originated in the Bronze Age. This detour is recommended if you have a real interest in antiquities but otherwise may prove an anticlimax.

Continue up the road beyond Vicarage Farm until it bends left, where a rougher track continues straight ahead. Follow this track, gently winding past fields, to meet another tarmac road. Turn left and go through the farmyard at Holme House. The road bends right and climbs before bending back left. Just after this bend go right at a footpath sign, up a field to a gate and stile onto the open fell.

4. The main path goes up right (for Fiendsdale Head and Langden valley), but we turn left. Cross a patch of rushes then traverse the fellside, slanting gently upward away from the wall. The ground is steep but not difficult. After about 200m, meet an obvious track in a groove and follow it winding uphill. At the next right-hand bend, leave the main track for a greener, less used, branch which climbs the slope overlooking the valley of Clough Heads Brook. Pass some pheasant pens and meet another stony track.

5. Turn left and follow the track, contouring along the flank of Hazelhurst Fell above a steep slope. There are splendid views over Bleasdale and Beacon Fell, with Preston and the West Pennines beyond. The most eye-catching features of the Preston skyline are the Deepdale football ground (home of Preston North End) and the tall, slender spire of St Walburge's church. Reaching 94m from the ground, it is the third tallest spire in Britain and the tallest on a parish church.

Follow the track, gently descending, until it dives away left down the side of a plantation. Continue straight ahead along less defined tracks following the upper edge of the plantation, with views now to west and north including Morecambe Bay and the Lakeland fells. The track eventually funnels into an angle of walls. Go down left then turn right to emerge to a road.

6. Turn left. This is Delph Lane and you could simply follow it back to the quarry, but to minimise road walking turn right after 30m on a track down towards Rough Moor farm. Cross a stile just above the farm, bear right, then follow a straight course through fields to meet another farm track. Go straight over and cross the next field to a gate just above a copse of trees. Head to the far top corner of the next field and through two gates to another waymarked route running almost parallel to Delph Lane. This takes you back to the quarry car park.

Above: The main climb, above Clough Heads Brook.. Opposite:The River Brock above Higher Brock Bridge..

Walk C8 Brock Bottoms and Beacon Fell

Full of surprises

Distance: 8.5km (5.3 miles)
Ascent: 260m (855ft)
Minimum time: 2½ hours
Underfoot: Riverside paths, fields, some lanes. Some damp areas.
Public transport: None available
Parking: Brockmill car park, near Higher Brock Bridge.
Public toilets: Beacon Fell
Refreshments: Beacon Fell
Maps: OL41
Start: SD 549 431

Beacon Fell is very popular. After the wilds of Bowland it may feel slightly sanitised, but that's Country Parks for you. It still has many merits, including a nice café – and some sudden, theatrical views through the trees.

This route makes a gradual, even circuitous, approach through the sheltered, wooded Brock valley and across rough grazing land. This way you'll feel you've climbed Beacon Fell, rather than just strolling up from the car park. As the descent begins you feel poised above the Lancashire plains, as if Beacon Fell is somehow far higher than it has any right to be.

The Walk

1. Cross Higher Brock Bridge, turn left at a footpath sign and keep left of all the houses to a gate and stile. Bear right through the field and cross a small stream before joining the riverside path. After 500m bear right (waymarks) and climb through the trees away from the river then turn left on a vehicle track, descending to a house (currently being restored). Bear right above the house on a narrow path along the edge of woodland. This has some elaborate boardwalks where it traverses above the river. A broader path leads to a path junction near a footbridge.

2. Don't cross but turn right, away from the river, up a track, which becomes a tarmac lane (obviously little-used). On a right-hand bend look for a well-hidden bridleway sign on the left. Follow the rough track down to a bend with a bench then bear right to a footbridge. Cross this and follow a path leading into the Waddecar Activity Centre (owned and run by West Lancashire Scouts but available to other groups).

   Follow the main track through the site, keeping below the steeper slopes. As the track runs out into fields, keep straight ahead to find a footbridge near the confluence of two small streams.

3. Don't cross the bridge but turn right, past a ruin, to a stile into woodland. Follow a clear path, which soon crosses a side stream and climbs beside it. Go left over a stile onto open ground carpeted in rushes.

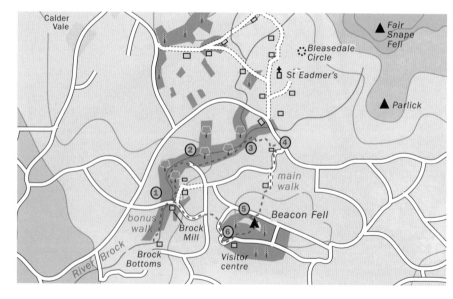

Top: Duckboards by the River Brock. Above: Start of the descent from Beacon Fell.
Overleaf: Fine woodland beyond Waddecar.

Follow waymarks and a broken line of trees; Parlick lies straight ahead. As a track develops, follow it right, over a stile, along a fence and then straight ahead to a gate and stile where footpaths meet. Turn right and follow frequent waymarks towards a recently converted barn and then around its garden and out to a lane.

4. Turn right along the lane. After a sharp right bend turn left on a track with the conifers of Beacon Fell now on the skyline. Keep straight ahead as the track forks, going through the entrance to Heatherway Farm. Opposite the house turn right over a stile, and follow a line of trees (mostly alder). After 90m turn left to a stile and go straight up to a road. Go right a short way then left up a slanting track through the conifers. Meet another track and turn left. The large wooden sculpture is the size of an alligator but I take it to be a newt. Beacon Fell has a number of sculptures, mostly carved in situ by Preston artist Thompson Dagnall.

5. Follow the level track past an open area then turn right up a rough path through trees and across heathery slopes to the 366m summit. There are good views to the north over Bleasdale although trees cut off much of the panorama. Continue straight ahead, across a junction of tracks and then bear right, soon descending to the Visitor Centre where there are toilets and a nice café.

6. Turn right along the road. On a right-hand bend, opposite a sign for Starling Wood Car Park, turn left and go down to a gate and sudden view west. Descend steeply to another gate and continue down in the same line to a stile and even steeper descent (some steps) through new tree plantings to a footbridge. Bear slightly left to a stile onto a lane. Go right 30m then left on White Lee Lane, which leads back to Higher Brock Bridge and the car park.

Bonus Walk: More Brock Bottoms

Distance 2.4km (11/2 miles)
Ascent: 60m (195ft)
This is actually the walk that most people do from the car park, and if you've time and energy to spare after doing the main route it's a thoroughly charming little extra, and keeps you rather more in touch with the river. Quite honestly it does not need detailed description: follow the obvious and well-trodden path downstream from the car park. After 1.2km the path forks and the left branch leads almost immediately to the ruins of a mill. This makes an obvious turn-around point.

It is also possible to continue downstream (after back-tracking to the fork). If some of the party have extra energy the rest could arrange to pick them up at Walmsley Bridge or even the next road crossing at New Bridge.

Opposite: Approaching Burnslack Brook in winter.

Walk C9 Burnslack, Paddy's Pole and Parlick

Variations on a classic theme

Distance: 14.3km (8.9 miles)
Ascent: 545m (1,790ft)
Minimum time: 4 hours
Underfoot: Fields, quiet lanes and some rough sections.
Public transport: Stagecoach bus 4 links Preston, Longridge and Chipping, Monday–Saturday all year. Bowland Transit bus B12 links Clitheroe, Garstang and Chipping on Thursdays only, late May–late October.
Parking: Main car park in Chipping
Public toilets: At car park in Chipping
Refreshments: Pubs and cafés in Chipping, but nothing en route.
Maps: OL41
Start: SD 622 434
Dogs: On leads throughout.

With Clougha Pike as well as Paddy's Pole, 'summits' that you reach by walking downhill seem to be a Bowland speciality. In fact Paddy's Pole is not a summit at all, but in every way that matters it roundly trumps the 'parent' summit (Fair Snape Fell). Perched above one of the steepest slopes in Bowland, it is the best of all viewpoints over the delicious bowl of Bleasdale. And from there to Parlick, the fliers' favourite, is the best ridge walk in the district.

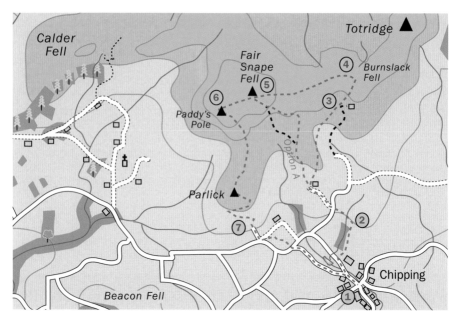

There are several good routes to Paddy's Pole, and this is one of the more devious, but this allows for a gradual and really rather lovely approach from Chipping, culminating in the hidden delights of Burnslack Brook. The penalty, especially after wet weather, is that the ridge path above the Brook has a few slutchy sections. But this is Bowland after all, and it makes you appreciate the good bits all the more. And there are a lot of good bits...

The walk is described starting from Chipping, which allows access by bus as well as making for a grand varied circuit. Those with cars can enjoy a shorter walk, less varied but only marginally inferior, by starting from the popular parking places on Startifants Lane, below Parlick. Follow tracks and footpaths past Wolfen Hall and Saddle End to meet the main route.

The Walk

1. Walk up the lane left of the church to a fork on the edge of the village. Go down and right past factory buildings new and old to pass a mill pond. Halfway along this turn right into a drive and immediately over a stile on the right. Go up the slope and follow the right-hand edge through a couple of small fields into a much larger one. Bear slightly left and find a small marker-post and thin path, which descends to run parallel to a stream. Cross a stile into woodland. Cross a footbridge and go straight up the slope to a gate just left of a house.

2. Enter the yard and turn left through another gate. Follow the obvious track until it meets a

lane. Go straight across and follow another farm track (Saddle End Farm). Go through the farmyard and turn right along a level track. (Or see option A).

Follow this track, sometimes climbing gently, until it runs out into a field. Just before the field, fork left on an indistinct track above the field wall and continue to the ruins of a farm on a slight shoulder, once known as Ward's End. There are many abandoned farms in Bowland but I always find this one of the most evocative.

3. From the ruin follow a fairly clear track down and along the valley floor – there are some moist patches. The valley narrows and curves away ahead, hiding what's to come. Indistinct paths continue above and parallel to the stream but on a good day when there's not too much water it's a delightful game to follow the watercourse itself as closely as possible, hopping from side to side as necessary. But tread lightly as this is a fragile place and please don't bring large groups this way (the path up Saddle Fell is the obvious alternative).

As the valley diminishes to the merest gutter, continue along the fence. The going gets tougher, with peat hags and wet patches. On meeting another fence turn left.

4. It's a tough call to decide which side of the fence is better. Staying to the left (south) looks promising at first but later on there seems more of a path on the north side. There isn't much in it but having tried both ways, I'm going on the north side next time.

After about 1km the path becomes clearer, with a route from Bleadale Water joining from the north. Soon there's a gate in the fence; if you've been on the north side, cross here, and

Above: Classic moorland walking above Burnslack Brook.

head south about 50m to another gate, where the route via Saddle Fell comes up. Go through the gate and follow a reasonably clear path back towards the fence. Negotiate some final peat-hags to reach a gate by a junction of fences. The highest point (520m) is the untidy cairn nearby, but the trig point and the usually accepted 'summit' – also known as Paddy's Pole – are 1km to the southwest across a near-level plateau.

5. Go through the gate and turn left along the fence; cross a transverse fence before bearing right to reach the cairn. Arriving at Paddy's Pole (510m), it's obvious why this is the preferred destination and why the OS surveyors preferred it too, as it sits close above steepening slopes that sweep down into Bleasdale.

6. Turn left along the edge of the plateau, which funnels into a narrowing ridge – probably the best in Bowland. Continue down the ridge to the neck and then up onto the summit of Parlick (you could sidle round left on a contouring track, but come on...).
Before the lowest point there's a curious rocky breach on the Bleasdale Side, known as Nick's Chair. It looks almost artificial, but 'almost' is probably the operative word. There seems to be no archaeological evidence of human construction here. However, with Bleasdale Circle (see Walk C7) in the valley just below, who can say for sure?

The descent from Parlick is wickedly steep; use the zig-zags both to protect your knees and to ease erosion. It's still a relief to roll out into the lane at the bottom. You might feel envious of the paraglider pilots who can just glide down – but remember, they've first had to climb it with a backpack that's unlikely to weigh much less than 20kg. And the occasional hang glider pilot will be carrying a load that's significantly heavier and much more awkward.

Parlick (a.k.a. Parlick Fell or Parlick Pike) is one of the most distinct and recognisable tops in Bowland. Projecting from the main mass of the fells, with steep slopes on three sides, it's particularly popular with paraglider and hang glider pilots. Parlick offers good launch sites and flying can take place in almost any wind except a northerly. It's considered the most important site in Lancashire; for more see the website of the Pennine Soaring Club at www.penninesoaringclub.org.uk/penninesites/parlick.htm. And in the valley below there's also a glider launching field operated by the Bowland Forest Gliding Club (www.bfgc.co.uk; open Wednesdays and Friday–Sunday). One way or another, on most days there will be someone soaring above, below or right alongside you.

The longest recorded flight from Parlick is 125km in a hang glider, landing at Hetton-le-Hole, just south of Sunderland and only a few kilometres from the east coast. The longest paraglider flight is 76km.

Right: The descent from Parlick, with the Loud valley and Longridge Fell beyond.

7. Descend the lane past a junction, then turn left over a stile beside a gate. Bear half-right (roughly aiming at Pendle Hill), cross a stile in a fence and continue down to another stile. Continue in a similar direction, gradually curving right to head downhill to a stile beside a gate just above a farm (Fish House). Don't be tempted by the footpath through the yard of the farm. This looks a good route on the map (via After Lee) but it's incredibly wet in almost all weathers. Instead turn left along the lane (a designated Quiet Lane) then fork right and just follow the road for about 1.5km down into Chipping.

Option A. This is shorter and easier but misses the hidden delights of Burnslack Brook. When the ground is wet many will feel this is a sacrifice worth making.

At Saddle End Farm don't turn right but continue straight ahead up a rising track. Follow this steadily up the fell, which becomes quite a well-defined ridge. Higher up, the track braids into several strands. Keep towards the left of these and eventually a better-defined track slopes off left towards a fence. Rather than crossing the fence here, follow it up about 200m to a gate about 50m short of the fence that runs along the main ridge (if 'ridge' isn't too flattering a term). Go through this gate to rejoin the main route.

Walk C10 Longridge Fell – a circuit from Hurst Green

Masses of variety and some really terrific views

Distance: 11.6km (7.2 miles)

Ascent: 280m (920ft)

Minimum time: 3¼ hours

Underfoot: field paths, heath and forest. Some of the forest paths in particular can be very muddy at times. Some road walking at the end.

Public transport: Hurst Green is served by bus service 5 between Longridge and Clitheroe, every couple of hours Monday–Saturday. There's currently no Sunday service.

Parking: Park considerately on Avenue Road, Hurst Green. The village hall car park is the best place (donations invited) but fills up when there's an event on.

Public toilets: Near the memorial at the road junction in Hurst Green.

Refreshments: Three pubs in Hurst Green. The village shop has closed. No refreshments en route.

Start/finish: SD 684 341: in front of the Bayley Arms Hotel on Avenue Road.

Map: OS Explorer 287 West Pennine Moors and OL41 Forest of Bowland & Ribblesdale are both needed for this walk.

It's C11 that gets the Tolkien hype, but fans of The Lord of the Rings may feel that there's just as much – maybe more – of the right ambience on this less fêted walk, which also gives a far more complete picture of Longridge Fell than the customary out-and-back route from Jeffrey Hill. I'm not suggesting that's a bad walk – Longridge Fell is far too good for that – just that this one is better.

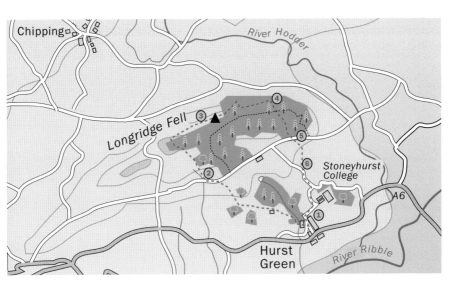

The Walk

1. Cross the road and bear right down a tarmac drive with footpath sign. Take a narrow path to the right of some garages, join a track and continue past two cottages to emerge alongside a stream, Dean Brook, which runs in a beautiful sculpted rocky bed. Go up slightly to join a wider track and continue to a small stone bridge. The surroundings hereabouts are delightful – and maybe a little bit Elvish?

Cross the bridge, go up steeply and then along a fairly level path, which runs into a track. Keep straight ahead past a tall old house (Greengore), built as a hunting lodge in the 16th century. A more open section, with a rougher path, gives the first glimpses of the conifer-clad upper slopes of Longridge Fell. Cross a stile by a metal gate to reach a junction of tracks. Don't take either of them but climb a faint path half-left up rough pasture. Cross a fence at the top and bear right over a rise and down to the far corner of the field. Continue diagonally through the next field to a gate leading onto a road.

2. Turn left for about 400m then turn right up a tarmac track with a sign for Dutton Dog-house. Walk straight up this track for 800m until it bends sharp right. Here go straight ahead on a narrow path which soon leads to a stile and Access Land sign. Continue up the faint path, roughly parallel to the fence (later wall) on the right, to another stile and sign. The direct route to Spire Hill bears right here but it's well worth a small detour for variety and better all-round views, so turn left immediately after the stile, following a narrow trod into an open stand of pine trees. There are wide views hereabouts over the lower Ribble valley. The

Left: Walking by Dean Brook.

reservoirs around Longridge are prominent and beyond them Preston and the Ribble estuary.

Stonyhurst College

Stonyhurst College is one of the country's leading Catholic boarding schools, with strong Jesuit traditions. The main college caters for boys and girls from 13 to 18 while the attached St Mary's Hall is a preparatory school, for those from three upward. Its most famous alumnus is Arthur Conan Doyle, creator of Sherlock Holmes, and the poet Gerard Manley Hopkins was once a teacher here. Stonyhurst also makes much of its connections with JRR Tolkien (see Walk 11). Originally the seat of the Shireburn family – a name also commemorated in one of Hurst Green's pubs – the estate was donated to the Society of Jesus (Jesuits) in 1794, becoming home to a scholastic community previously based in Belgium (but composed mainly of English expatriates). Its main chapel (one of six) also serves as the village Catholic church. The grounds are usually open throughout July and August, the house – with its Elizabethan core – from late July to the end of August (closed Fridays). There are also several public ootpaths crossing the grounds, including part of walk 11.

The path is hard to trace through the pines but it doesn't matter as the going is easy. Keep near the right edge of the stand of trees and at the end bear right to the corner of a fence, which encloses dense plantations of spruce. Step over the dilapidated fence to join a sandy path and follow this, with the plantation on your right.

Cross a stile, with a stone wall just beyond. Turn right: there are paths both sides of the wall, but the going is generally drier if you stay this side. Continue past a bend in the wall and up the final rise to Spire Hill, the summit of the fell at 350m. Cross a handy stone stile to the trig point and a grand view north over the Loud valley to the main mass of the Bowland Fells. It's pretty Tolkien-ish too, if you ask me – in fact I'm off to start an Internet rumour that Spire Hill is a mis-spelling and should really be Shire Hill.

3. Stay on this north side of the wall now, for the best views, until it bends left. Cross a stile then go left on a descending path, almost tunnelling through the trees. It's sometimes muddy, and always stony, generations of travellers having raided the old wall alongside for a firmer footing.

Eventually the path kinks right through a gap in the wall (white and yellow waymarks on a post), rises a little then swings back left. It's always the clearest route. Follow it out to a junction with a clear forest road and turn left. Enjoy the easier walking for a stretch and, in summer, the range of flowers in the verges – eyebright, selfheal, bird's-foot trefoil, and many more.

Follow the track over the slight rise of Hare Hill and on to a junction. Bear left (almost straight ahead) on a more overgrown track, soon leading to a clearing with another fine view northward – and some handy logs to sit on.

4. Continue just a few paces then turn right on a narrow but clear footpath. Follow this to meet another wide track, turn left a few paces and then right at a footpath waymarker. Follow the narrow path, parting tall bracken in summer, to a fork at another waymarked post. At time of writing the left-hand route – the one indicated as a right of way – is overgrown and if you persevere you only end up stymied by fallen trees. These relatively new waymarks suggests someone may have plans to clear the route, but at present the only viable option is to take the right fork. This is very muddy in places (I suppose it might dry out in a drought) but at least the route is trodden and obvious.

Follow it down to a stone wall running across your way. Turn left for 50m to a gap. The public footpath comes down to this point; there's another new waymark but few signs of traffic. Turn right through the gap then follow a narrow path trending left, to emerge above an old quarry with a blue pool in the bottom. Keep left of the hollow then slant down beside tall trees to a stile and the road.

5. Turn left for 20m then go right over a stile. Go down the field to a stile then bear left, aiming for a gate just left of a house (Fell Side Farm). Join a track then go straight down, between the buildings, and down into a dip where a track develops. Follow the intermittent track, with a stream on its left, to emerge to a lane by a cottage.

6. Go left down the lane, passing Stockbridge Cottages, to a junction. Turn right. The next 400m stretch is a bit busier and lacks decent verges, so take care. The lane passes a golf course before emerging to a set-piece view of Stonyhurst College. Turn right, following the road away from the school – no lack of verges here! The road climbs slightly then kinks left near a statue on a pillar (known as the Lady Statue, it was erected in 1882, and is inscribed 'Ave Maria'). Pass a small cemetery and re-enter Hurst Green, where the imposing Shireburne Almshouses overlook the road. The village hall car park is just beyond – and so's the pub.

Above: The sculpted rocky bed of Dean Brook

Walk C11 Three Rivers — hunting for hobbits

A well-worn and well-loved route, and none the worse for that

Distance: 10.6km (6.6 miles)
Ascent: 175m (575ft)
Minimum time: 2½ hours
Underfoot: Grassy field paths, farm tracks and some woodland paths.
Public transport: Hurst Green is served by bus service 5 between Longridge and Clitheroe, every couple of hours Monday–Saturday. There's currently no Sunday service.
Parking: Park considerately on Avenue Road, Hurst Green. The village hall car park is the best place (donations invited) but fills up when there's an event on.
Public toilets: In the centre of Hurst Green.
Start/finish: SD 686 389
Map: OS Explorer 287 West Pennine Moors

This is often referred to as the Tolkien Trail, but I have to register a degree of scepticism (see The Tolkien Connection, after the walk description). This little corner of Lancashire may or may not have had a major influence on Tolkien's depiction of the hobbits' homeland, The Shire. For devotees of The Lord of the Rings it's fascinating to examine these possible links. For the rest of us, it's a pleasant diversion and if the play of the imagination adds to the pleasure of the walk, all to the good. And anyway, even if you don't care a fig for Tolkien, it's still a very pleasant walk.

Purely in a spirit of fun, I'll mention in the walk description a few correspondences that suggest themselves to me – all are from The Fellowship of the Ring, the first book of the trilogy.

The Walk

1. From the memorial in the centre of Hurst Green, walk down to the left of the Shireburn Arms and through the car park to a stile. Follow a hedge downhill then continue beside a small stream to duckboards and a footbridge into woodland. Go over a rise, then down a steep path with wooden steps to emerge near the Ribble. Go left to a stile then walk along just above the river. Loop past the end of an aqueduct bridge and continue near the riverbank, eventually meeting a gravel track.

Pendle Hill looms in the distance – some have suggested this as inspiration for the Misty Mountains, but this really is pushing it... It's also been offered as the original of the Lonely Mountain but this is central to The Hobbit, published long before Tolkien's visits to Lancashire. If it's anything, surely it's Weathertop (Book 1 Chapter XI).

2. Follow this track where it bends right at Jumbles. Jumbles Rocks is one of several shallow places in the river where fording would appear to be possible (but you try it at your own risk). Ford of the Bruinen? (Book 1 Chapter XII).

Continue along the track until it goes through a gate and starts to bend away from the river, then bear right to rejoin the river bank, and follow it round a big meander. On this side of the water is the Boat House, once a ferryman's cottage; the ferry ran to Hacking Hall – obvious on the far bank. It remained in operation until the 1950s so Tolkien would have known it well and it is a good bet for the original of Bucklebury Ferry (Book 1 Chapter IV). Remains of the ferry can now be seen at Clitheroe Castle Museum.

Just above Hacking Hall, the River Calder joins the Ribble. Continue along the riverbank, joining another track. Follow this for about 800m to a point opposite the confluence of the Ribble and the Hodder. A screen of trees means this could be missed, but it's just before a gateway, where steps

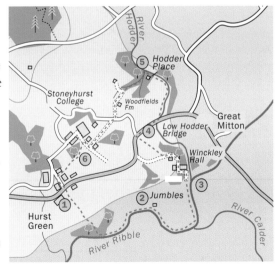

Left: Looking across to Hacking Hall, at roughly the point where the ferry once ran.

run down to the water. Here the Ribble comes in on the far side and the walk now continues alongside the Hodder. Follow the track to Winckley Hall Farm.

3. Turn left towards the farmhouse then right between barns. Bear left past a pond and into a lane, which climbs quite steeply before levelling out and swinging left. Go through a kissing gate on the right near a derelict building (probably old pigsties) and straight across the field to another gate. Keep straight ahead across the next field, left of a wood which hides the river below. Drop down past a pond and continue to a road.

4. Turn right down pavement to the river, looking out for the remains of an ancient bridge on the right.

This is known as Cromwell's Bridge – for the ironic reason that its parapets are supposed to have been smashed on the orders of Oliver Cromwell to speed up the passage of his army's baggage train. The bridge was actually built in 1562. There are many bridges in The Lord of the Rings, one which definitely lacked any parapets being the Bridge of Khazad-Dum (Book 2 Chapter V).

Just before the road crosses the Hodder, turn left along a track that runs close to the river. The placid shallow waters are a popular attraction for local families on hot summer days. Eventually the track climbs up below the high walls of Hodder Place, once a preparatory

Above: Cromwell's Bridge over the River Hodder

The Tolkien Connection

It's true that The Lord of the Rings author JRR Tolkien did visit the area several times during the years 1942–47, staying in a guest house owned by Stonyhurst College (where his son was a teacher), and probably writing some of the trilogy in a room in the school. He would have walked most of the footpaths in the area, so there can be little doubt that on this walk you are following in his footsteps. It's also been observed that the map of the Shire in The Fellowship of the Ring, the first part of the trilogy, bears some resemblance to this part of Lancashire. One of its three rivers is called the Shirebourn, only one letter away from Shireburn; the Shireburn family were the original founders of Stonyhurst and one of the pubs in Hurst Green is the Shireburn Arms.

Having said all that, a few counter-arguments should be recognised. First, Tolkien began writing The Lord of the Rings in 1939, three years before his first known visit to the Ribble valley. What's more, it clearly follows on from his earlier tale, The Hobbit, published in 1937. Second, the primary inspiration for the Shire is undoubtedly the rural West Midlands, especially Worcestershire, where Tolkien lived for most of his boyhood. Much of the landscape he knew then was subsequently swallowed up in the industrial sprawl of the Black Country – this, along with his experiences in combat in the First World War, are fairly clearly the sources of the orcish devastation of Isengard and Mordor. Third, Humphrey Carpenter's definitive biography of Tolkien makes no mention at all of Stonyhurst or of Lancashire. Fourth, the Shire map does not really bear that close a resemblance to the Ribble valley. For instance, its two lesser rivers (The Water and the Shirebourn) both join the main river (the Brandywine) from the west. Here, the Calder enters the Ribble from the east. The Shire map shows many rolling hills or downs, whereas the geography hereabouts is dominated by the single spine of Longridge Fell. And so on.

It seems clear to me that Hurst Green and its surroundings can't be the primary inspiration of the Shire. However, the Shire is never named in The Hobbit and its geography is scarcely developed. The maps in the book do not cover it, but there is a detailed map of 'A Part of the Shire' in The Fellowship of the Ring. It's quite possible that – consciously or unconsciously – Tolkien absorbed much of the landscape and atmosphere of the Hurst Green area during the years when The Lord of the Rings was being written; a large part of its attraction for him may have been that it reminded him of the lost landscape of his boyhood.

One thing is for certain, and worth remembering now a new generation has come to know The Lord of the Rings firstly from Peter Jackson's magnificent trilogy of films. These were produced in Jackson's native New Zealand – somewhere Tolkien never visited. Though born in South Africa, for most of his adult life he travelled relatively little and rarely outside Europe. The roots of Middle-Earth are ultimately English.

school for Stonyhurst, now converted to apartments. Immediately descend again to a stone bridge.

5. Turn left up a track beside the stream to reach a footbridge. There's definitely a 'Tolkien-ish' atmosphere in the woods here but I've never tied it down to any specific location. Climb wooden steps then follow a narrow path along the top edge of the woods until it crosses a stile into a field. Continue along the field edge then cross a stile into a stony track. Go straight ahead to a farm (Woodfields) and out to a road. Turn left a few metres then right down a track. Follow this to Hall Barn Farm and along the right side of the buildings.

6. Turn right on a tarmac track for 200m. (For a closer look at the impos-

ing facade of Stonyhurst College, continue straight ahead, then return to this point). Go left through a gate by the end of a wall (if you're returning from the detour turn right). Walk along a narrow field, with sports pitches to the left and woods on the right. Bear right near the end on an emerging track alongside the wood then go up to a kissing gate. Follow the field edges through two more kissing gates into a narrow path. This leads to a short lane. At its end turn left, back to the centre of Hurst Green.

Above: The side-valley after Hodder Place. Opposite: The View from near Hodder Heights.

Walk C12 Hodder Heights and Crag Stones

Another parade of varieties

Distance: 10.6km (6.6 miles)
Ascent: 274m (900ft)
Minimum time: 3 hours
Underfoot: The regular mix of lanes, tracks and rough moorland paths.
Public transport: Bowland Transit B10/B11 bus from Clitheroe/Slaidburn, Monday–Saturday.
Parking: One or two spaces near Newton Bridge but do not block access; there's a parking area on the Slaidburn road out of the village.
Public toilets: None
Refreshments: No refreshments en route.
Maps: OL41, Harvey
Start: SD 698 503

The beaky profile of Crag Stones is prominent from the Hodder valley, but until the Right to Roam arrived there was no legal route of access; it was one of my first destinations after the fells were opened up. After long anticipation, it could have been a disappointment, but it wasn't.

Crag Stones may be the high point – literally and figuratively – but the journey is not just about the destination, and this walk has some fine passages from the opening (and closing) riverside fields to rough (but never too rough) moors before and after Marl Hill.

The Walk

1. Follow the riverside path downstream from the bridge. Before the field tapers to nothing, cross a wall and then follow the top of a steep bank above the river. Continue until the river makes a definite swing to the right; here bear left to a gate. Hold the same heading through two more fields to emerge to a lane near a house (Foulscales). Turn right.

Walk along the lane about 200m then turn right on a tarmac track. Follow this till it bends left and then forks. Take the left fork and follow the track to its end at High Birkett.

2. Keep straight ahead through the farmyard, left round the end of a barn and then right again on a rougher track in the same direction as before.

ollow the track to a ford, straight ahead a few metres then take the left fork as the track splits. The track curves slightly rightward before petering out. Keep straight ahead across open moor. A wall on the right comes in to meet you, then turns sharp left. Cross a stile then bear left on a path descending gradually into a valley. Cross the stream and climb the other side where it's marked by some obvious ridges that look like old spoil heaps.

3. Leaving this chaotic ground a clearer path develops, crossing a side stream then bearing left up the moor. Go straight up to a stile and continue alongside a wall, pass left of a cow

Above: Crag Stones and the Hodder Valley. Right: Distinctive boulder near Crag Stones.

shed and meet a road. Turn right, pass Marl Hill and drop down towards a stream. Just before the bottom turn left over a stile.

4. Follow vague paths until the fence on the right bends left. Cross at a stile and continue along a path (that sometimes feels more like a drainage ditch).

Clearer paths join from the right and then a prominent isolated boulder makes a good landmark. From this follow a path, roughly parallel to a wall off to the left, down to a small bridge in a dip. From this bear left towards the wall to cross at a stile. Continue just left

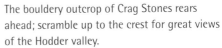

of the wall, then bear left to cut off a corner, ford a stream and again walk parallel to the wall.

The bouldery outcrop of Crag Stones rears ahead; scramble up to the crest for great views of the Hodder valley.

5. Return to the path and continue, bearing left down a wall. Cross at a gate, from which go straight ahead over a slight rise to a stile. Bear left to a footbridge then walk near the fence, with the stream on your left, down to a track. Turn right and follow this track for about 1km. It winds down past a barn, crosses a sizeable stream and then makes a sharp right turn.

6. At this point go left over a stile on a public footpath. Follow a hedge on your right through two fields then go down an enclosed track to meet tarmac by a house (Gibbs). Go down the drive to emerge on the lane at Foulscales, opposite the footpath of the opening stages, which is retraced back to Newton.

Walk C13 Croasdale, upper Whitendale and Dunsop Head

Right at the heart of Bowland, and well worth its position

Distance: 12.3km (7.6 miles)
Ascent: 570m (1,870ft)
Minimum time: 3¼ hours
Underfoot: Good tracks and rougher moorland paths.
Public transport: There is no public transport nearer than Slaidburn. To link to the described walk route, walk up Town End (past the Hark to Bounty) then take a footpath on the right just past the last houses. Follow this to Myttons and follow the access track to Wood House Lane: turn right and walk up to the end.
Parking: A few scattered parking spaces at the end of Wood House Lane, above Slaidburn (follow signs for Myttons Craft Centre then continue to the end of the lane). Park considerately and do not block access.
Public toilets: In Slaidburn
Refreshments: No refreshments en route.
Maps: OL41, Harvey
Start: SD 693 548

Slicing across the main Bowland ridge, the Salter Fell Track is a tantalising challenge to every walker, but in its entirety it's a long trek and better suited to a linear walk (see L2) – and if you ask me it's better still by bike (see M4). However this walk is a neat solution to the problem, taking in the southern half of the legendary track, then dipping into the unjustly

unfrequented upper reaches of Whitendale. The third leg of the triangle is the crossing of Dunsop Head, a grand bit of Bowland moorland walking. For a mid-length route, which includes no actual summits, this is about as good as it gets.

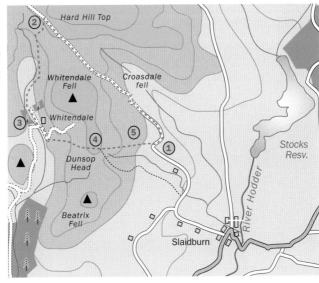

The Walk

1. Go through the gate at the end of the lane and follow the obvious stony track, known variously as the Hornby Road, the Salter Fell Track or Salter's Way, contouring round the hillside to run above Croasdale. The track remains obvious and it would take an exceptional talent to get lost. Descend slightly to New Bridge and then climb steeply past some old quarries before the track resumes a more gradual ascent. About 4km from the start, go through a gate and enjoy the first views to the north west, over the upper reaches of Roeburndale and out to the ragged skyline of the Lakeland fells.

2. Follow the track, descending gently, for another 800m to a signpost and a narrow path descending to the left. Follow this path, swinging further left lower down. The way is narrow but always clear enough, and the path is mostly firm, though a few patches remain soft in all but the driest of weather.

   The path traverses steep slopes just above the Whitendale River for about 1km before easing away from the river over more open slopes. Aim for the gap between two small plantations then bear right down the pasture beyond to join a clear farm track. Follow this to the cluster of buildings at Whitendale.

3. Pass the main farmhouse and bear left on a tarmac track. Go up through a yard beside cowsheds and through another gate onto a rougher track.

   Swing right and zig-zag up the steep slope, continuing more easily past swathes of cotton grass (in summer). The path is sometimes stony, sometimes peaty and has short stretches of duck-boards. The way becomes vague for a short distance approaching the wall that runs across the top of the fell. Bear slightly right here and gently downhill to a gate in the wall at Dunsop Head.

Left: Pastures in middle-Whitendale.

4. Once through the gate, an obvious path goes right, almost parallel to the wall, but the route we want goes almost straight ahead. Unfortunately the path is almost invisible at first and the ground is wet, but a clearer track emerges within no more than 250m. To find it, walk directly away from the gate for 80m, then bear slightly right, keeping higher peat hags away to your left. Descend slightly to cross a stream, beyond which the track should be visible. Another useful landmark is the end of a wall ahead, where it meets a fence. The track passes about 100m right of this, and by this point is eminently clear and firm underfoot.

5. Having located the track, the rest is simplicity itself as the track runs a fairly straight course, slanting down a steepening hillside, to meet the Hornby Road just above the fell gate.

Above: Upper reaches of Whitendale. Right: The summit of Pendle Hill, looking towards Colne and Nelson

Walk C14 Pendle Hill

So very steep and high: the highest point on wholly Lancastrian ground

Distance: 11.8km (7.3 miles)
Ascent: 490m (1,605ft)
Minimum time: 2¾ hours
Underfoot: Clear and mostly well-drained paths throughout except for a short stretch of open moorland after Point 4.
Public transport: P70/71 Pendle Witch Hopper links Clitheroe, Barley and Nelson. 70/71 Sunday service – from Easter–October – is a circular route also including Burnley and Padiham.
Parking: Large car park on the outskirts of Barley.
Public toilets: At car park
Refreshments: Pub and tea room in Barley.
Maps: OL41
Start: SD 823 403

Many Lancashire people will tell you that Pendle Hill is the highest in the county. They're half right. The highest point in the county, not counting the top of the Winter Hill radio mast (778m), is at 628m on the lumpy ridge of Green Hill, on the border with Yorkshire. At 577m, however, Pendle is all ours, and a worthy champion; not just the highest but one of the best. Unlike pretty well every other significant hill in Lancashire, Pendle stands out in splendid isolation, figuring prominently in views from every direction and always recognisable.

Naturally Pendle has history. It's famous (or infamous) for its witches; eight women and

two men were tried and hanged at Lancaster in 1612. The story was dramatised in Harrison Ainsworth's novel, The Lancashire Witches (1849) and again in Robert Neil's Mist Over Pendle (1951), a classic which has never gone out of print. More recently still, Lancashire witchery is the theme of Joseph Delaney's The Wardstone Chronicles, which began with The Spook's Apprentice. This is now 'in development' in Hollywood, though that's no guarantee we'll actually see a movie made any time soon, let alone that it will be filmed in Lancashire.

In perfect contrast, Pendle also played a major part in the birth of the Society of Friends, or Quakers. Forty years after the witch trials, George Fox was in Lancashire. Later he wrote in his Autobiography:

'As we travelled we came near a very great hill, called Pendle Hill, and I was moved of the Lord to go up to the top of it; which I did with difficulty, it was so very steep and high. When I was come to the top, I saw the sea bordering upon Lancashire. From the top of this hill the Lord let me see in what places he had a great people to be gathered.'

Soon after this, Fox spoke to a gathering of a thousand or more on Firbank Fell near Sedbergh in Westmorland (now Cumbria) – a spot still known as Fox's Pulpit.

The Walk

1. From the toilets follow a path rightwards across the green then over a footbridge. Turn right up the street. Pass Meadow Bank Farm then turn left up a footpath alongside a stream.

Above: On the main climb up Pendle Hill's Big End.

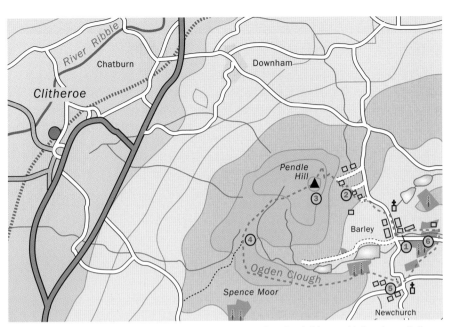

Follow a well-worn path through a field then cross another footbridge and join a lane. Follow this, with lots of signs, to a kissing gate and a well-marked path, which leads up to a house (Brown House).

2. Go into the yard, bear right on a track for 50m, then left through another kissing gate. Follow the path down and right, then ascend through new plantings and straight up a field to a gate left of a farm (Pendle House). Bear right and up to a kissing gate. Climb straight up on a remade path, which soon swings right and climbs the very steep slope by a staircase of large blocks. As the gradient eases there's a wall and a fine stone marker post. Go back left above the steep slope, joining a well-worn track to the trig point, standing on a hump, which may be a Bronze Age burial mound.

The top is a sprawling plateau, which restricts the views westward, but the eastern half is great. The valley of Pendle Water is directly below. The Yorkshire boundary – and the Pennine Way – run across the first range of hills to the east. Further north is a lower green expanse, crossed by the rivers Ribble and Aire, and then the Yorkshire Dales National Park. South are Colne, Nelson and Burnley and then more hills, half in Yorkshire, half in Lancashire.

3. Bear right, across bare ground, soon joining a path of massive stone slabs. Follow this down to a stream (Ogden Clough), cross, and go left along a narrow path which traverses the steep slope above the beck. The path broadens as it runs out onto more open slopes, as Ogden

Clough bears away left. Go up slightly to a large cairn where the path becomes level again.

4. Bear away left on a broad ridge. This is basically trackless but the going isn't too bad (not by Bowland standards anyway!). Slightly right of the highest ground a wall comes up from below. Aim to meet this near its highest point and as it starts to descend again it's crossed by a public footpath. Follow this left, almost level. The path is sometimes vague but it's a line to follow. The way becomes clearer as the ridge narrows, clearer still as it follows the edge of a conifer plantation (Fell Wood). Continue along a fence and wall to a signpost and bear right, keeping roughly level until the rooftops of Newchurch appear. Aim for a water trough, then a stile and signpost. Descend a short path to the road.

5. Go down the road opposite, signed for Roughlee, for 100m. Cross a stile on the left and follow a rising path; enter a plantation then fork left. At the far end keep straight on, gradually converging with the wall on the left. Follow the wall, changing sides halfway, to a sunken track. Go straight across and descend to a road.

6. Go down the tarmac track opposite, cross the river then go left alongside it. Continue on a stonier track past cottages and an old mill. Where the track bends back to the road, a short path on the right leads back to the car park.

Above: Descending to Newchurch. Opposite: Descending Rodhill Lane.

Walk C15 Bolton-by-Bowland and Sawley

A pastoral symphony

Distance: 9km (5.6 miles)
Ascent: 210m (690ft)
Minimum time: 2 hours
Underfoot: Mostly fields, paths sometimes faint.
Public transport: C2 bus from Clitheroe visits Sawley and passes Point 7. Hourly, Monday to Saturday.
Parking: Small car park on the edge of Bolton-by-Bowland beside Skirden Bridge.
Public toilets: At car park
Refreshments: Pub in the village and another at Sawley, just off the route.
Maps: OL41
Start: SD 784 494

This walk is more Ribble valley than Forest of Bowland, but there's nowt wrong with that. And it does climb high enough for some fine all-round views, while Pendle Hill is a constant brooding presence as you descend back to the valley. The walk route itself only grazes the edge of the two villages, but both are well worthy of further exploration.

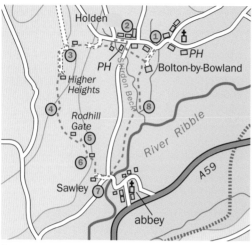

The Walk

1. Turn left out of the car park, cross the bridge and turn left again on a tarmac drive beside the sports field. Follow this drive to a left-hand bend, at which go straight ahead to a sign-posted stone stile. Cross this and turn right to a kissing gate. Follow the well-waymarked route across fields then take a narrow path left of agricultural sheds and out to the road. Turn right and walk to the Copy Nook pub then turn left on a lane signed to Holden.

2. In the hamlet of Holden fork left (signed to Lane Ends). Cross a bridge then turn left on a tarmac drive. Ignore the footpath bearing left across fields and stay on the drive until just before the house then go right on a narrow path beside outbuildings. Continue in the same direction up a couple of fields to a stone stile onto a track. Go straight ahead over another stile and up a field, parallel to a fence with a track on its right. At the top of the field go through a gate to join the track.

Where the track levels out, with a farm (Fat Hill) in view ahead, bear right on a stony track through a gate then continue in the same direction as before. Fork right again onto a vague grassy track which runs a few metres right of the farmhouse and up to a gate. Follow the track ahead into another field and find a stone stile in the corner close to another farm (Priest Biggins).

Cross the stile and follow the right edge of the field, and the next, to another stile which leads to a tarmac track on a ridge, where the views expand dramatically.

3. Turn left and follow the track to a farm (Higher Heights). Fork right on a stony track along the back of the farm buildings. Go straight ahead through a gate to follow a

stone wall on your left, which abruptly ends by a superfluous stile. From this bear slightly left (if clear, aim for the highest point of Pendle Hill). There's no path, but follow a level course and then descend into the furthest corner of the field. Cross two stiles and follow the obvious groove and intermittent line of trees along the contours.

4. The groove begins to bear left and descend and becomes more obviously an ancient track (Rodhill Lane). It's shady, stony and often slippery as it cuts directly down the slope before emerging beside a house (Rodhill Gate). The bridle-way continues directly ahead, along a line of trees and through a small wood – slippery and nettle-ridden in summer. It may be preferable to join the tarmac drive on the left, which is a public foot-

path; follow this down until it zigs left and back right just above another house; the bridleway emerges from the wood here.

5. Go through a gate ahead, directly below the wood. (If you followed the bridleway down, turn right immediately on leaving the wood). Follow the lower edge of the field until you can cross through a metal gate on the left just beyond a tree. Continue in a similar direction until you can drop down left to a footbridge. Cross this, climb the steep slope and follow the right edge of the field towards a line of conifers. Go through a gate at the right corner of the plantation then follow its edge along and round to the left. Go through a gate into a farmyard.

6. Leave immediately through another gate on the right. Follow a track, with the fence on your right, down into another field. The track becomes very vague but follow its line just above a belt of woodland on the left to locate a stile at the end of the field about 20m right of the corner. The stile looks unpromising but just a few metres into the wood a much clearer

Opposite: Flowery pastures on the ridge. Above: Bolton-by-Bowland.

path is encountered. Turn left on this, and go down steps in a garden to reach a tarmac lane beside a Friends Meeting House. This looks out, very appropriately, towards Pendle Hill (see C14 for more about the Quaker connection).

7. Meet a road, turn left and then bear right on a busier road towards Sawley Bridge; beware of speeding traffic here. To visit Sawley Abbey and/or the Spread Eagle pub, cross the bridge and follow the road, which makes a sharp right turn by the pub; the abbey entrance is 150m further on. To continue with the walk, turn left on a footpath before the bridge (if returning from Sawley, turn right after the bridge). Follow a well-trodden and waymarked footpath across fields, briefly running close to the Ribble. Keep straight ahead, leaving the river, and cross more fields before a waymark points right to a footbridge over Holden Beck.

8. Cross and turn left, climbing onto a narrow neck of land between Holden Beck and Skirden Beck. Follow waymarks and a trodden path then cross a track and go through an old iron kissing gate under copper beech trees. Go straight ahead then follow a fence on the right that encloses woods dropping steeply to Skirden Beck. Cross another stile to continue along the

edge of the wood then keep straight ahead as the wood edge turns further right: aim about 25m right of an isolated tree to find a stile rather hidden in the hedge.

Continue straight ahead from this towards another isolated tree, below which is the stump of a stone cross, then drop down left into the corner of the field to the stone stile which was crossed early in the walk. Retrace the opening stage along the tarmac drive back to Bolton-by-Bowland.

Top: Beside the Ribble on the return leg from Sawley. Above: Sawley Abbey. Opposite: On the ridge of Whelp Stone Crag, with Pen-y-Ghent in the distance.

Walk C16 Gisburn Forest, Whelp Stone and Bowland Knotts

Some tough passages link some inspirational highlights

Distance: 17.7km (11 miles)
Ascent: 470m (1,540ft)
Minimum time: 5¼ hours
Underfoot: A real mixed bag, from forest roads to near-pathless moorland
Public transport: Nothing really convenient, but possible access from Tosside on the Slaidburn–
Settle route via Bailey Lane.
Parking: Stocks Reservoir car park (a.k.a. Vicarage Garden), Gisburn Forest (free of charge).
Public toilets: None.
Refreshments: Nothing en route.
Maps: OL41, Harvey (the route just strays off the Harvey map north of Whelp Stone Crag)
Start: SD 732565

This is a hard walk to sum up, with a massive contrast between the forest confines and surfaced tracks of the early stages, and the raw moorland and vast prospects of the middle section before rough tracks and field paths usher in a gentle unwinding back to the shores of Stocks Reservoir. Despite the nearby presence of the man-made forest, and a road crossing later on, there's a real wild feel to the middle part of the walk, and the rocky ridges of Whelp Stone and Bowland Knotts are a delight.

84

The Walk

1. Leave the car park by the vehicle entrance and bear right on a path parallel to the road (red and blue waymarks); where it bends away, cross the road then continue on another path, still parallel to the road, until you meet a broad forest track by a gate. Turn left, and follow the track, which is soon joined by the main mountain bike routes; there should be plenty of room for everyone but groups of walkers should not walk more than two abreast, and watch those extending dog leads! The track, known as Eggberry Road after a farm that once stood here, runs through a valley, with mostly natural woodland masking the ranks of conifers.

2. Pass a short track down to the right. Soon the main track forks; the narrower right branch runs through a sort of cutting, but this is a bike route, so continue a little further on the main track then go right and down to a footbridge, meet the bike track again and then follow a narrower path which runs close to Bottoms Beck. When the two tracks rejoin, keep straight on, then cross the beck on a concrete bridge.

Follow the track uphill, swinging round right then passing between fields and approaching Hesbert Hall. Just before the track enters the forest again, turn left on another track which climbs more steeply to a junction. Go right about 50m then turn left on a faint path alongside a tumbledown wall.

3. The path becomes a little clearer as it slices through the forest, before meeting another forest track. Keep straight ahead and descend a little to the edge of the forest where there's a shed and a storage tank. Bear left just before the shed, following a waymarked path across rushy ground and then alongside a wall and wire fence. At the end of the fence follow waymarks to change sides and continue along the wall.

Cross a rough forest track and keep following the wall; it's probably best to return to its left side at first and walk along a slight ridge running parallel. When this line is blocked cross the wall again and continue to a stile and the first view of Whelp Stone Crag. Follow a faint path across open moor parallel to the forest edge, eventually drifting away from it to avoid a very wet area. The natural line now appears to be straight up to the rocky summit, but I would recommend working back left above the wet area to meet the wall again at some rocks below

Above: Pools near the crossing of the Keasden Road

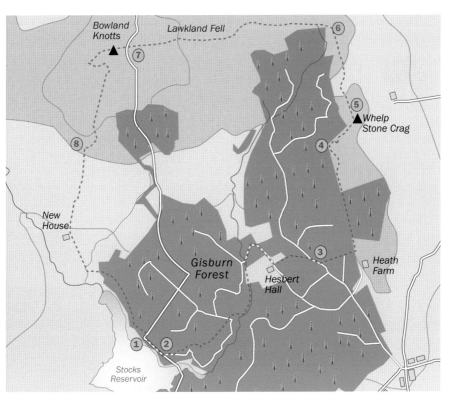

a stand of pines. This area gives good views of the highest part of the mountain bike trail (see p148), and the rocks, trees and broken wall make great foregrounds for photos over the forest to the main Bowland ridge.

4. Scramble up between the broken crags to the summit trig point and discover that it's not just an isolated knoll but a fine little ridge, fringed with crags, which runs away north east, aiming exactly for Pen-y-Ghent. Follow this ridge, picking up a wall then passing through a gap, from which bear left towards another rocky rise.

Drop down from this keeping left of the jumble of boulders that forms its north ridge, then continue across open ground in the same direction to join another broken wall bounding the forest. Follow faint paths roughly parallel to the wall, crossing one transverse wall in poor repair. Just before another crossing wall, slip through a handy gap and then cross a stile and go through an old gateway onto open moor.

5. Follow a vague path towards a curious dark hollow where the peaty soil is exposed. The bed

of the hollow is fenced off and very wet, so skirt round to the right then cross the stream above the fencing and bear left again towards the corner of the forest and a conspicuous flat boulder called the Resting Stone. There is indeed a handy shelf on its southern face where you can rest your load.

6. The obvious course from here would be to turn west along the forest edge but there are some unnecessary ups and downs and some of the dips are very wet, so contour round the first dip and then head due west along a vague ridge. The paths are equally vague but the going is easy. For no apparent reason this nondescript little rise bears the name White Swan. Cross a slight dip (a bit damp) and then onto another rise with the much more descriptive name of Brown Bank. From the top of this bear slightly left and look for the place where quad bike tracks find a reasonably solid route across the marshy dip.

Go up a broad slope alongside a deep gully and as this fades go straight up, picking the best line between green mounds of moss and deep heather. Cross a level shelf with a couple of drainage channels then bear left to rejoin the wall as it rises to Knotteranum (what a name!). The summit is on the wrong side of the wall, though, and there's nowhere to cross but we'll just have to give this one a miss. Continue along the wall to rise once more onto Bowland Knotts and the Keasden Road.

7. From here the easy route is to turn left down the road for about 100m then bear right on an obvious track (footpath sign) but a better plan is to continue on a track just north of the wall for about 500m then cross it near a sharp bend to reach the trig point (430m). I wouldn't recommend a direct link from here to the track as the ground between is very wet. The safest bet is to swing round left, just below the crags, and contour round to meet the track. If conditions generally aren't too wet you could also go half-right (SW) from the trig point to cross a stream, from where you should find quad bike tracks heading almost due south and then bending left to meet the main track.

However you reached the main track, it's obvious when you get there, with deep ruts (and usually big puddles). Follow it until it swings slightly left and through a gateway before splitting. Keep straight ahead, just left of some deep grooves in the moor, then turn right near the corner of a wall and follow a green track directly downhill until it swings right to a junction.

8. Turn left on a narrow green path; watch out further down as there's some subsidence. A gate leads into pasture. Bear right down towards a barn among tall trees, meeting a clear track leading to a gate and stile.

Right: View from the high moors to Stocks Reservoir and Pendle Hill.

Swing left by a newly-restored well, near a waymark for the Stocks Reservoir Circular Walk. Follow the track steadily downhill, with more waymarks, until it crosses a stone bridge over Hasgill Beck. Bear left up to a gate and then follow the waymarked path straightforwardly back to the car park. You'll see several signs of former habitation here, including the former vicarage garden, now a picnic area, which gives the parking site its official name.

Bonus walks

There are several waymarked walking routes in the forest, which are well-waymarked and can be followed without a map or detailed instructions; there's an overview map on a board in the car park. The 'White' walk is an easy 2.1km, the 'Blue' is 3.5km and the 'Red' is 5.3km. The opening stages of our route follow the first part of the Red route.

There is also a circular walk around Stocks Reservoir; this doesn't simply trail round the shoreline but loops out into the upper valley of the Hodder, meets the road near Kenibus and coasts pleasurably round Esk Hill before looping back across the dam and along the southern shore. It's well waymarked and easy to follow, and leaflets with maps and outline description are generally available from a dispenser at the car park.

Walk C17 Roeburndale

Explore one of Bowland's least-known valleys.

Distance: 12.9km (8 miles)
Ascent: 420m (1,380ft)
Minimum time: 3½ hours
Underfoot: Quiet lanes, farm tracks, field and woodland paths.
Public transport. The nearest bus service is at Wray (80/81/81B). Walk down Main St and turn right up School Lane. Continue, climbing almost continuously, for 1.7km to a junction with Moor Lane. Turn left to reach the cattle grid and parking place.
Parking: Turn off the B6480 at Butt Yeats (Moor Lane, signed for Roeburndale). Small parking area immediately beyond the first cattle-grid, where the lane reaches access land; there's a small plantation on the right.
Public toilets: None
Refreshments: No refreshments en route.
Maps: OL41
Start: SD 599 657

Roeburndale is easy to get to, yet feels remarkably remote. The magical woods at Mallow Gill are a real highlight, but there's plenty more to relish, be it meadows glowing with buttercups in summer or wide views across to the Yorkshire Three Peaks on a crisp winter's day.

The Walk

1. Walk along the road for approx 1km. There is a path of sorts on the moor running parallel, but the road is easier, has little traffic and equally fine views. Turn right at a footpath sign on the track to Thornbush, go straight through the farmyard and turn right at the end of the buildings. The track enters a field and goes left but the right of way goes straight ahead up the slope in a shallow depression. Turn left along the fence at the top to rejoin the track above a line of trees and go right. Follow the track through another gate into a field where the walls make an acute angle.

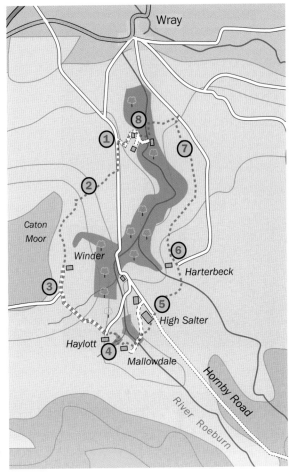

2. The track now follows the right-hand wall: leave it and walk straight ahead, splitting the angle between the walls. As you start to descend look for a stile in a stone wall ahead. Cross and descend past a way-marked post into the valley of Warm Beck. Cross at stepping stones and follow the obvious path out on the other side but just before it reaches open slopes scramble up right to another marker post.

Follow the indicated course across rushy ground, aiming to the right of trees seen ahead. Go over a slight rise and down to the angle of two fences where there's a field gate, kissing gate and a track running ahead. Follow the track, which crosses another beck and passes just left of a dark spruce plantation. Keep following the track to pass a farm (Winder) and meet a tarmac road.

3. Turn left through a gate marked Public Road (you can see why this needs to be made clear!). Follow the road down and up again to a farm (Haylot). Where the road makes a sharp

Opposite: Views over Roeburndale in the early stages.

left, go right a few paces then left at a footpath sign in front of the farm. Go through a gate into the field on the left and bear right down to the bottom right corner. Go through another gate and down the narrow enclosure to a stile at the bottom right. Follow the field edge, with steep woods on the left, until another stile leads to wooden steps and a narrow path descending through the woods to a bridge over Mallow Gill.

4. Climb the steep slope beyond and skirt left of a small larch plantation; continue up the slope aiming left of farm buildings (Mallowdale). Follow waymarkers skirting the farm then cross a small bridge and stile onto the access track. Descend this to a bridge (Mallowdale Bridge) and up the other side, passing a barn as the track levels out. Just before a cattle grid turn right, cross a stile and go up the left edge of a meadow to a gap just left of a prominent stone barn (High Salter).

5. Turn left on the track past the farmhouse then bear right at a footpath sign along a rough track. As this fades, keep near the wall on the left, descend to a stile and turn right to another stile. Cross the next pasture diagonally to find a stile in a wire fence just left of the opposite corner. Continue towards a metal gate in stone wall; don't go through but bear left along the wall to a stile in the next corner.

From this go half-right across rushy pasture (aim towards Whernside, if you can see it, and well to the right of the next farm). Locate a stile where a wooden fence meets a wire one and continue along the wire fence until you can see a footbridge in the surprisingly rocky valley below. Cross the bridge, go over a stile and bear left on a grassy rake. This leads to a stony track which goes via a ford (clapper-bridge alongside) into a farmyard (Harterbeck).

6. Turn right to leave the yard and immediately left on a stony track. As this bends left go through a kissing gate and follow the fence. Go through a gate to another track and bear right. Cross a stile just left of a barn and bear right near the field edge to a stile just left of the corner. Cross onto rough grazing and follow a vague path past an isolated hawthorn and along a

tumbledown wall. Continue in a similar direction, now with better-maintained walls on the right.

Pass a small pool; a marshy area on the other side of the wall marks the former site of Wray Wood Moor Tarn. From the next gate follow the track between walls then keep straight ahead to meet a surfaced track near the hamlet of Outhwaite.

7. Turn right briefly then turn left over a stone stile. Cross a small stream (sometimes just a marshy runnel) and continue gently downhill with the stream on your left. Cross a wooden stile, then a stone one. Turn left to a gate and stile and follow a rough track. (If you need to return to Wray, turn right after the stone stile then turn left on the lane). The track bears right and becomes vague, crossing meadows to a gate into woodland. Descend the track, swinging left, to emerge into the open at the bottom. Bear right to a footbridge.

8. Cross and go up steps to a track near old sheds. Turn left on the track, meet another track on a bend and bear right uphill. The track bends back right and then left: here a steep path goes straight up the slope. Turn right on the track above and follow it through woodland and round left through Backsbottom Farm. This is part of the Middlewood Trust and organic produce is often on sale. Continue up the track to the road and turn right a short distance back to the start.

Opposite: Warm Beck. Above: Near the site of Wray Wood Moor Tarn.

Walk C18 Lawkland Moss

The very edge of Bowland, and a very distinctive walk

Distance: 7.8km (4.8 miles)
Ascent: 145m (475ft)
Minimum time: 2 hours
Underfoot: Mostly fields, some lanes, and a stretch of wetland (not unfeasibly wet if you stick to the route).
Public transport: The bus service to Lawkland was withdrawn in 2006. Clapham station is about 3km from Eldroth – and 3km back! A better bet would be bus services along the A65; disembark at the Falconry Centre and walk down the lane alongside (Crow Nest Road) to a right-angle bend. Go straight ahead on a footpath across fields to Lawkland; just over 1km from the A65.
Parking: Park considerately in Eldroth; the best places are outside the village hall.
Public toilets: None
Refreshments: No refreshments en route.
Maps: OL41
Start: SD 763 654

This hardly feels like Bowland at all, as the land tilts towards the edge of the Yorkshire Dales. The outlook is almost always to the east, with Ingleborough constantly thrusting to the front of the crowd shouting 'look at me!' It's largely a pastoral walk but it's the undrained wetlands at Lawkland Moss that make it a bit special.

The Walk

1: From the village hall walk into the village (i.e., if you came out of the village hall car park you'd turn right). Turn right on a track (sign for Rigghead) which soon passes under the railway (the line to Carnforth and Lancaster). Follow the track past one house until it ends at Rigghead. Go straight ahead through a gate and follow a wall on your left. Where the wall bends away keep straight ahead through an open field with a little stream valley down to the right. As the field narrows, go left over a stile near a power-line pole. Bear right through a scatter of boulders, with a wire fence on your right, to a stile in a stone wall. Cross the stile, turn left and follow a farm access track out to a lane.

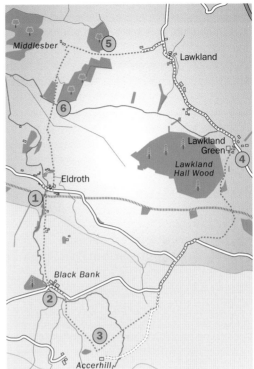

2. Bear left along the lane for 50m then right on a track with a footpath sign. Go through a dip then follow the wall on your left until it turns a corner. Continue straight ahead along a vague path beside a ditch, over a stile and bear slightly left in the next field to a gate. Go up another field, with a wall on your left, then go left over a stile near some outcrops of rock.

3. Go straight down a long field, near a wall on your right, to a rough stile; just beyond this is a slab foot-bridge over a small stream. Keep the same heading over rises and dips, then look out for a walled hollow on the left where an otherwise subterranean stream is revealed. Continue to a gate and bear left along a lane (Stackhouse Lane). Keep straight ahead as a wider lane comes in from the left and continue through a sort of crossroads (its right arm is a rough track).

As the lane bends right, take a track almost straight ahead. Follow it down to a bridge over the railway and wind through fields to a ford (footbridge just to the right). Continue up the track, keep straight ahead through a farmyard and join a lane; bear left. This is Lawkland Green.

4. Follow the quiet lane for about 1.5km. There are good views of Lawkland Hall, a fine Elizabethan house with some lovely gardens behind (visits only for groups by prior arrangement). A

Opposite: Walled hollow in the fields before Stackhouse Lane.

little further on, on the right, is the impressive Bank Barn, one of its lintels bearing the date 1763.

Continue into Lawkland, another tiny hamlet, and turn left just after the phone box and (now defunct) bus-stop sign. This track appears to end beside a house but its line continues as a sunken, rushy groove under trees. Walk down beside it to a gate with waymarks going in two directions. This is Lawkland Moss. Attempting to follow the left-hand path can lead to all sorts of bother so go almost straight ahead (dog-legged slightly to the right) and through a strip of rushes and tall grass flanked by woods. A straight course leads to a waymarked stile.

The going is relatively easy but there is a sense that this is an untouched landscape, or at least not 'improved' like most of the land round about. This is very much how most of the lower ground in this region would have been before mosses were drained and forests cleared. This is Access Land so you are free to explore, but it's easy to get turned around in the dense woods with frequent swamps, pools and creeks. (Translation: we did!).

5. Keep going generally straight, with several more waymarks, until just before some farm buildings. Turn left and walk along a field edge to another gate; beyond this is more unimproved mossland. Go through the gate, turn left for 20m and then right again along a vague but straight path through lush vegetation. Reaching slightly higher – and drier – ground, bear left (more waymarks) and soon right again, following the edge of a wood. At the end is a stile almost hidden under trees, and then a footbridge.

6. Cross another stile and head across the field to the far left corner, near tall pine trees. Go left, over a stile, then turn right (there's a stone stile beside a gateway). Go up to a stile on the skyline. Walk down to a gap stile in a transverse wall and straight on down to a corner of a wood. Follow its edge down to a gate in the corner of the field and follow waymarks through a garden out to a lane. You're back in Eldroth, opposite the track to Rigghead. Turn right and you're soon back at the village hall.

Above: Ford and footbridge near Lawkland Green.

Linear Walks and a Circular Tour

Why linear walks? Sorry, wrong question. The right question is: why not?

Think about it. It cannot possibly be the case that all good walks start and finish in the same place. Looking at the map, some natural circular (or 'horseshoe') routes may suggest themselves, but Bowland is also full of linear features – ridges, valleys and established tracks–crying out for a different approach.

Linear walks have something extra: a linear route is a journey. What's more, linear routes can take you further for the same effort. Consider the difference between the Longridge Fell circuit C10) – excellent though it is – and the Clitheroe–Chipping walk (L4), which also crosses the Fell.

Okay, the latter is a bit longer, but it takes in a much greater variety of country and places Longridge Fell in its context hill; the circuit is a much tighter examination of just one aspect. The circuit is a grand walk, but the traverse is a much more complete one.

This is not about whether you use public transport or not. You can use public transport to access most of the circular walks, and you can do the linear walks by car with a bit of jiggery-pokery (usually involving two cars or a non-walking driver). Using public transport is a good thing and often the most convenient way to do these walks, but it is not their raison d'etre. They are in this book because they are great walks.

Still, I have aimed to ensure that all the walks described here can be done using bus and/or train services. There's something of an exception in the case of the Hornby–Slaidburn route (L2) but this really comes into its own as part of a longer tour (see below). The other five are all straightforward to complete using public transport and make fine days out.

However, the routes haven't just been conceived in isolation. They also combine into a continuous loop through and around the Forest of Bowland. See the following page for more about doing them as a continuous tour.

Using public transport

Unlike some linear routes, none of these walks start or end in the middle of nowhere. If you arrive at the end and there's an hour to wait before the next bus or train, there's a handy pub or cafe to wait in. However, it often makes sense to avoid such waits entirely, by doing the bus/train journey before the walk. For instance, if you're doing the Clitheroe–Slaidburn walk, base yourself in Clitheroe (yes, that could mean parking the car there) and get the bus to Slaidburn first. That way you can walk back to Clitheroe with no background worries about when the last bus goes.

Details of bus and train services are based on 2010 timetables. There's no reason to think they will change drastically in 2011, but it's always a good idea to check before making a special journey (see Further Information at the back of the book).

Caton to Caton – The Tour

This tour is specifically designed so that each stage ends at a centre with good choices of food and lodging. They also have good transport links. Doing the tour in the described order, i.e. starting from Caton (or Lancaster) is suggested because of its ease of access and also because this leaves the toughest (and arguably the best) day till last. It's described in six stages but can readily be shortened to five by combining two of the shorter stages; either 3+4 or 4+5. It's also possible to devise a more direct route between Slaidburn and Chipping (see below), but the two are not easily linked by public transport so it's less convenient as a day walk. Anyway, it's a pity to miss Clitheroe and even more of a pity to miss the fine walking over Easington Fell and Longridge Fell.

There are several possible routes from Slaidburn to Chipping, and both the North Lancashire Bridleway and the Journey to the Centre of the Kingdom make this link. But personally my choice would be to take the pleasant and well-trodden valley route to Newton, then the first half of C12 to Marl Hill. Follow footpaths from Crimpton to Whitewell and cross the stepping stones below the Inn at Whitewell, then go via New Laund, Higher Fence Wood and Dinkling Green to Lickhurst, then finish by the North Lancashire Bridleway.

Accommodation

The smallest bases used are Slaidburn and Chipping, where options are naturally most limited and booking ahead is particularly advisable. When booking accommodation, make sure that it is actually in the destination town/village, or otherwise near the walk route. Beware the establishment that proclaims itself 'five minutes from Slaidburn'; this will mean five minutes by car, not on foot. If booking through a tourist information centre make sure they know you are travelling on foot.

Descents

As with the circular walks, I've given an estimate of total ascent for each walk. However, being place-to-place routes, a couple of the walks end up lower than they started. In these cases the total descent is also indicated.

Ruins of Fell Side, with Pendle Hill behind.

L1 Caton—Hornby

A riverside walk par excellence

Distance: 13.4km (8.3 miles)
Ascent: 50m (165ft)
Minimum time: 2¾ hours
Underfoot: Riverside walking thorough fields and woods. Some sections can be quite muddy in winter/wet spells.
Public transport: Lune Villager services 80/81/81/81B from Lancaster, half-hourly Monday to Saturday. Sunday service hourly.
Parking: At Crook o'Lune or by the river in Hornby.
Public toilets: At Crook o'Lune.
Refreshments: Woodies snack bar at Crook o'Lune. Several pubs and village shop in Hornby. Nothing in between (none to be found by detouring into Aughton or Gressingham either).
Maps: OL41
Start: SD 522 647

The luscious Lune valley may not seem like quintessential Bowland, but the entire walk from Caton is within the AONB. With its broad flood plain, looping meanders and steep wooded bluffs, this stretch of the Lune is right out of the geography textbook. As a day walk it is a fine mix of pasture and woodland; as a first leg of the tour it may feel more like a preamble, with the dark Bowland skyline constantly hovering in the south. With its largely level walking it is also a good leg-loosener before the sterner fare of Day 2.

The Walk

If arriving by bus, disembark in the centre of Caton. Walk down the short road left of the post office to meet the Lune cycle-path; turn left and follow it to Crook o'Lune.
Opposite the car park entrance are bike racks and picnic tables, not to mention an 'artist's easel'. Walk down past these on a path that loops back right into the trees. Turn left down steps to the river bank and go left again, heading upstream. Follow the path along the banks, looking across to Low Mill. Continue past a weir and into a wood.

Emerge into the open again. The way crosses the middle of the field to a footbridge. Easily missed in the woods on the left is a small waterfall. Continue to a handsome bridge. This was built in 1881 to carry water from the Lake District to Manchester. Both of the low paths under the bridge can be very muddy and it's sometimes easier to go up and over the bank instead.

Continue into another wood and follow the main path through it. This is a prime spot for bluebell-lovers in season. Towards the end the path becomes narrower and traverses steep slopes with some steps, finally dropping down to a stile. Skirt a fallen tree and continue

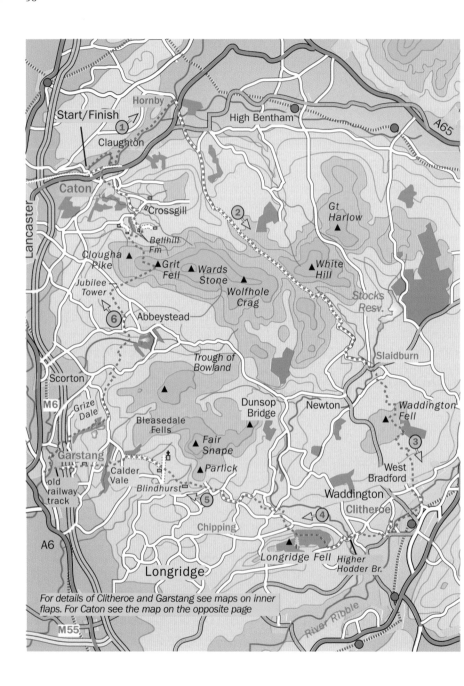

Start/Finish
Hornby
Claughton
①
High Bentham
A65
Lancaster
Caton
Crossgill
Bellhill Fm
Clougha Pike
Grit Fell
Wards Stone
Wolfhole Crag
②
Gt Harlow
White Hill
Stocks Resv.
Jubilee Tower
⑥
Abbeystead
Trough of Bowland
Slaidburn
Scorton
M6
Grize Dale
Bleasedale Fells
Dunsop Bridge
Newton
Waddington Fell
③
Garstang
old railway track
Calder Vale
Blindhurst
Fair Snape
Parlick
⑤
West Bradford
Waddington
Clitheroe
④
Chipping
A6
Longridge
Longridge Fell
Higher Hodder Br.

For details of Clitheroe and Garstang see maps on inner
flaps. For Caton see the map on the opposite page

M55
River Ribble

parallel to the river. Here the river makes a big loop, and the right of way follows it. It's awfully tempting, but illegal, to take a short-cut across the relatively narrow neck of land. This would save nearly 2km of walking – but the legal route does take in some fine riverside scenery.

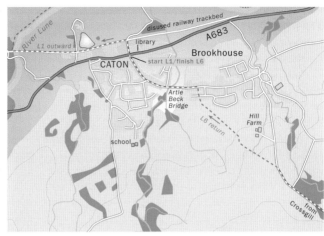

Slant slightly away from the river as the way turns back to the west, following Lune Valley Ramble signs over a small footbridge and across the next field. (I have found the path completely blocked by tall maize here. In this case the only course is to follow the right edge of the field). The path returns to the river bank, swinging back to a southerly and then an easterly heading.

Opposite a large barn (Over Lune Barn) waymarks take you left, away from the river, past the barn and over a stile. Keep following the waymarks, trending right. The route follows an obvious change of level, which is the former river bank. 19th-century maps show the river following this course.

As the river straightens out, a track develops parallel to it. Follow this, passing metal sheep pens, and continue to meet a tarmac lane (at Aughton Barns).

Leave the lane almost immediately over waymarked stiles on the right. Cross fields, following a straight course over more stiles, to meet the river again. The slightly elevated standpoint gives a good view upstream towards Ingleborough. Note also that there is a smaller side-channel on our side of the river; in fact there are a couple of islands here. Aim left of these, descending through rough, rushy pasture to a stile where the path enters another wood.

Keep following the path. It's narrow, can be a bit overgrown in summer and is often muddy, but there's never any real doubt about the route. It runs through the wood, then follows an elevated section of bank past a small fishing hut and enters more woodland. Emerging into fields again, follow the bottom edge, passing just left of a house to meet a track. Turn right and join a tarmac lane.

After 200m, as the lane rises, fork right through a gate by a signpost and go down to the flood plain again. Turn right to go straight across this, past a large pool. Aim right of a rickety-looking hut to locate a stile and turn left, parallel to the river. Continue upstream, passing the confluence of the Lune and Wenning, to meet a farm track (below Sandbeds). Soon leave the track again to find a gate in the corner of the field, and another woodland path. Follow this to a footbridge leading to open fields. Aim for the right edge, just above the river, and follow it for about 800m. A stone bridge (Loyn Bridge) can be seen ahead, with a wall tapering down to its left. Aim for the left end of this wall to find steps leading up to a road.

Turn right, cross the bridge and continue along the road. Take care on the bridge and the first section of road as it's narrow. It lacks verges and far too many drivers lack consideration. On the left above the bend in the road are the mounds of Castle Stede, a motte and bailey fortress which once guarded the river crossing.

It's possible to join a footpath on the right, which follows the river downstream and then turns up the banks of the Wenning into Hornby, but this more than doubles the distance from Loyn Bridge to the bus-stop. Following the road seems more logical; bear right when you meet the A683, which leads past several interesting buildings, notably the parish church of St Margaret with its unusual octagonal tower. Crossing the bridge over the Wenning there's a fine view over a curving weir to Hornby Castle. Most of what you see is Victorian or later, but it's built around a mediaeval core.

For those heading back to Caton or Lancaster, the bus stop is outside the Hornby Institute, another handsome little building (Grade II listed) dating from 1916 and designed by the famous Lancaster firm Austin and Paley. It's an important centre for village life, now boasting an IT suite alongside the original reading room.

The River Wenning and Hornby Castle.

L2 Hornby–Slaidburn

A classic ancient fell track

Distance: 22.9km (14.2 miles)
Ascent: 695m (2,280ft)
Minimum time: 6 hours
Underfoot: Quiet lanes and a fine moorland track; some fields at the end
Public transport: Reach Hornby by Lune Villager services 80/81/81/81B from Lancaster, half-hourly Monday–Saturday. Sunday service hourly. Slaidburn is on Bowland Transit B10/B11 service to/from Clitheroe, B1 to/from Settle, Monday–Saturday. No Sunday service.
Parking: Car park by the bridge in Hornby
Public toilets: At Crook o'Lune
Refreshments: Nothing between Hornby and Slaidburn.
Dogs: On leads on Salter Fell.
Maps: OL41
Start: SD 585 683

The meat of this walk is the same Salter Fell Track as used on MTB ride M4, but footpaths are used in the closing stages.

This is not quite the longest stage of the tour, but it is the hardest to split, and the least amenable to use as a day walk. You can shorten it a little by getting a bus to Wray instead of Hornby, but be aware that to get back from Slaidburn to Lancaster is a four-stage process: bus to Clitheroe, train to Blackburn, train to Preston (or bus Clitheroe–Longridge, Longridge–Preston), train or bus to Lancaster. It's theoretically feasible, but excessively long-winded. It's possible, of course, to do the two-car trick or get someone to drive round for you, but if you simply want to experience the Salter Fell Track on a day walk, C13 takes in a good chunk of it. Of course it's easier still to do it by bike, and this is by far the best way to do the track as a day outing. Unlike the others, this walk only really makes sense as part of the longer tour.

The Walk

The easiest way to get to Salter Fell is to follow the road (see description of Ride R1 from Hornby, but follow the lane through Roeburndale to its very end). Once out of Hornby the traffic is light and after the first climb the views are terrific. This road can also be reached from Wray; walk down Main Street then turn right up School Lane. Turn left at a T-junction, joining the road from Hornby. Continue to the very end of the road at High Salter.

If you'd prefer to avoid the road walking, try this: leave Hornby's Main Street by a signed footpath just left of the Hornby Institute, down a farm track, ahead through a short belt of woodland then alongside more woods. Follow a fairly straight line through more fields then alongside the obvious course of an old railway to meet a crossing track. Turn right on this. It briefly runs near the river then angles away and leads straight ahead into Wray. Turn left on the B6480 then right on Main Street. Pass School Lane (unless you want to switch to the road route) and continue until the road crosses the river. Immediately after this turn sharp right and walk up this road for about 2km until footpath signs on the right lead into a small triangular field.

Find a narrow stone stile in the left corner and then follow field edges. You're now following Walk C17 in reverse. Follow this past the site of Wray Wood Moor Tarn to the yard of Harterbeck farm. Keep reversing C17 over the ford/clapper-bridge and the next footbridge in its pretty rocky valley. Another kilometre across rough pastures leads to High Salter and the end of the road. Honestly, it would have been easier to follow this all along.

From here on there's no ambiguity. An obvious track continues from the public road, bending left out of the farmyard. Notice the North Lancashire Bridleway markers and a sign stating that it's 18km to Slaidburn. After a slight dip at Salter Clough the track climbs pretty steadily, and a grassy surface makes the going very pleasant. I hope you get a good day for this as the expanding views are really inspiring. On a bad day the sense of isolation is palpable but at least there's one consolation: you can't possibly get lost.

The surface becomes stony as the track climbs higher, then after a gate there's a more level stretch where the first southward views appear, with Whitendale snaking away below (see Walk C13). Continue more easily to a gate more or less at the highest point (416m).

The track begins to descend and soon twists steeply down past the remains of old quarries. Keep following the main track down, ignoring any branches: the main route is always obvious. Finally go through another gate onto tarmac at the start of a public road (also start/finish of C13).

Follow the road down for approx 2km; it's normally very quiet. Turn left at the signed entrance to Myttons Farm. Follow the drive into the yard then go right along a walled track into a field. Turn left along the field edge, go through a gate at the end then bear right on a trodden path to cross a small stream, follow the path briefly poised above a larger stream (Croasdale Brook) then continue across the field into woodland. Follow the path down to meet the lane again on the edge of Slaidburn and turn left into the village.

Quiet lane in Roeburndale.

L3 Slaidburn–Clitheroe

Keeps on delivering right to the end

Distance: 14.5km (9 miles)
Ascent: 365m (1,200ft) Descent: 425m (1,395ft)
Minimum time: 3¾ hours
Underfoot: Farm and moorland tracks, fields, riverside paths and a little road walking.
Public transport: Slaidburn is on Bowland Transit B10/B11 bus from Clitheroe, B1 from Settle,
Monday–Saturday. No Sunday service. Clitheroe has wide connections.
Parking: Clitheroe Park and Ride.
Public toilets: Near Council Offices in Clitheroe, next to bus stop in Slaidburn.
Refreshments: Nothing between Slaidburn and Clitheroe apart from the 3 Millstones Inn, just
off route in West Bradford (closed Monday and Tuesday).
Maps: OL41
Start: SD 714 523

If the previous walk is hard to figure as a one-day standalone, this is just the opposite. And the
bus journey from Clitheroe to Slaidburn, if circuitous, is a fine scenic experience in itself (those
big windows really help). The walk is essentially a journey from the Hodder to the Ribble,
crossing the pleasant ridge of Easington Fell. It has to be said you can't miss the cement works
as you drop down to West Bradford – it's all too prominent in most views of this reach of the
Ribble valley. But you can forget it again on the last leg along the river, with its extra
ingredient of some intriguing sculpture. And then there's Clitheroe, one of the most attractive
small towns in Lancashire – if you do nothing else here, give yourself time to walk up to the
Castle on its toothy limestone knoll.

The Walk

From the car park in Slaidburn (where the bus stops) turn left along the road and cross the
bridge. Pass one footpath sign then turn left at the next, up the drive to Poor'sland Barns.
Poor'sland Trust is a charity founded in 1621. Go straight ahead through a gate then slant up
the hill to a small gated stile on the skyline. Rejoin the road and go down right a short way
then left at another footpath sign. Follow a well-worn route up the slope. It's less clear as the
ground levels out, but converge with the wall on the right and follow it along until it bends
left. Cross a stile next to a metal gate and continue with another wall on your left. Pass a
plantation then cross the wall and continue, now with it on your right. Descend to a narrow
lane (used on Ride R4).

Go straight ahead into a surfaced track. Follow this to a T-junction by a stream, turn right
then left over a bridge. Bear right on a short track to a gate then across the corner of a field

to another gate. Go up the blind slope ahead, slightly right of centre, then descend to the right-hand corner. Don't use the obvious little footbridge and stile but go right through a gate, ford a small stream then cross a larger one on stepping stones. Go up left to a small gate then follow the left-hand fence to meet a track just right of a house (Skelshaw).

Cross to another obvious track and follow this, climbing gently, past a cowshed and up to another house (Fell Side: how do they think of these names?).

Go into the yard, observing the warning notice on the gate and bear left to the continuation track. When it forks go right and resume climbing; at all succeeding forks the main track is obvious.

The track climbs onto open moor and eventually reaches the crest of an ill-defined ridge. The quarries on Waddington Fell are obvious to the eye not far ahead – and to the ear too if it's a work day. Look for a large untidy pile of stones, known as Old Ned. A very faint path goes left from this towards another pile of stones called The Wife. (In mist this path could easily be missed: if you can't see The Wife, continue on the main track until you meet another track, then go sharp left). Just beyond The Wife meet another track and turn left.

Cross a wall at a metal stile (watch the middle rung on the far side) and continue along the path, soon descending through an old gateway and round some 'lumps and bumps' overgrown with heather. These look like old workings, forerunners of the present-day quarries. Bear right down a wider track alongside a conifer plantation, with good views to Pendle Hill somewhat marred by the cement works. After 250m go through a gate and turn right on another obvious track. Follow this about 500m then turn left through a gate onto a much narrower path descending towards a ruined house. This is another Fell Side – but quite a contrast with the last one.

The path runs straight until the slope steepens, when it makes an acute zig-zag to left and back right. Below this the original line is now a wet gutter filled with rushes; walk beside it down to a steep bank above a stream and bear right until the stream course opens out. Ford the stream – or find a dry crossing just below – then go back up left to a gate. Continue straight ahead with a wall on your left, then a fence as the track becomes clearer. Keep straight ahead on joining a tarmac track, go over a cattle grid and bear right on a lane.

Go through a sunken section and past a farm (Brocklehurst); 100m further on go right at a bridleway sign. Aim for the first power-line pole then follow an old bank and ditch to a gate. Bear half-left from this down to another gate. Follow the short track then bear right to the end of a hedge. Continue in the same line to meet a stony track just above a farm; turn left down the track between the buildings and down to a road on the edge of West Bradford.

It's impossible to ignore the cement works on the approach to West Bradford. The Castle Cement plant, now part of the Hanson Group, has been controversial for many years, with recurrent claims that it is responsible for atmospheric pollution and even an unusual cluster of cancer cases in one small area of Clitheroe. There was a successful prosecution relating to sulphur dioxide release in 2002.

Opposite: Above the old workings at the start of the descent from Waddington Fell.

Turn right along the road, over a bridge and then turn left on a green track (footpath sign). Follow the narrower continuation path beside the beck until it leads out to the road again. Follow the road (care) to Bradford Bridge, cross and then go right, over a stile with a Ribble Way sign. Follow the well-trodden riverside path, into Crosshill Quarry Nature Reserve. On leaving again through metal gates bear left up a slope then follow the tarmac path (keep left at each fork). Go left up a road. Pass a cemetery, turn right on a track then left through a gate. Follow a well-worn path across the field to the next gate, then turn left through another gate. These fields are the wettest part of the whole walk so it's sometimes better simply to stay on the road (turn right after the railway for the station and the centre of town).

Join a lane on the edge of town and go left. Walk down between terraces then turn left. The station is on the right, with direct access to platform 2. For platform 1, buses, or the rest of the fleshpots of Clitheroe, continue until a low bridge leads under the railway.

Clitheroe

Capital of the Ribble valley, Clitheroe is a bustling small town. Its history stretches back at least to Saxon times, and the name is thought to derive from Anglo-Saxon words meaning 'Rocky hill'; this would certainly suit the abrupt knoll on which the castle stands. Its Norman keep is one of the smallest in the country, but it is a very confined site. The whole of the castle site has recently been regenerated, with major improvements to the Castle Museum and the addition of a fine new café/restaurant. At the other end of Castle Street, my favourite building in Clitheroe is the 'flat-iron'-shaped Public Library – which has previously done duty as Town Hall, police station, lock-up, and public lavatories (not all at the same time)!

Clitheroe's roots are largely agricultural but it grew rapidly during the Industrial Revolution, with 13 cotton mills at its height. Limestone quarrying and associated industries are also important.

L4 Clitheroe–Chipping

A walk of three parts, all of them enjoyable

Distance: 16.2km (10.1 miles)
Ascent: 400m (1,315ft)
Minimum time: 4¼ hours
Underfoot: Mostly fields, some lanes, some rough paths on Longridge Fell.
Public transport: Clitheroe has wide bus and rail connections. Chipping has a bus service (4) to Longridge and Preston (almost hourly Monday–Saturday); Longridge also has connections to Clitheroe and Blackburn. B12 runs between Clitheroe, Chipping and Garstang on Thursdays in summer – one bus each way.
Parking: Park and Ride car park on Chester Avenue, behind the station.
Public toilets: Near Council Offices in Clitheroe; at car park in Chipping.
Refreshments: Edisford Bridge is the only stop en route, too early to be much use. Chipping has several pubs and two cafés.
Maps: OL41
Start: SD 742 419

This is largely a low level walk across green pastures, but there's a sharp change of tone in the middle as the route climbs onto Longridge Fell. A blanket of conifers limits the views from the ridge, but there's a fine prospect back over the Ribble valley from the crest of Birdy Brow before you enter the forest, and later the Loud valley makes a grand dramatic entrance. An intricate route then takes you on to the picturesque village of Chipping.

The Walk

If you arrived by train from Preston, Blackburn or Manchester, simply exit the platform and turn left on a footpath leading into a back street. From the opposite direction, or from the bus stops, go under the railway and turn left on the same footpath. From the car park head towards the railway then turn right just before the bridge.

Turn right on Kirkmoor Road. At the end continue into Back Commons, then go right through a kissing gate and across fields on a well-trodden path. Go along a line of trees to another kissing gate then take the fainter left path and follow it round left to enter a yard and then join a track (Ribble Way markers).

Keep straight ahead as the track enters a street, go past a converted Wesleyan school and then turn sharp right and down to a turning circle and footpath sign.

Cross the Ribble on a fine wooden footbridge and turn left on a lane. Meet the B6243 and turn right. It's busy and uncomfortable for a short way. Pass the Edisford Bridge pub then turn right – signed for Bashall Eaves and many other places. Walk along here 250m to a footpath sign on left.

Cross the field diagonally to a gate and stile, bear right up the field edge then follow waymarks across the green lawn of the Edisford Flying Club (model aircraft) and keep straight ahead, aiming directly for Longridge Fell. Keep just left of the hedge through more fields to a road and turn left.

Keep straight ahead at a junction and descend past the former Hodder Bridge Inn, now housing, to Higher Hodder Bridge. Cross this then turn left up a lane signed for Hurst Green and Longridge. This is the main climb of the day and the near-constant gradient makes it easy to find a rhythm. Just below the top the road bends sharp right then more gradually back left. Take the track on the right here, starting at a gap between a gate and a short wall. (Though it's worth detouring across the road and going up a short rise for the view back towards Clitheroe and Pendle Hill).

The track is not a right of way but access is permitted by the landowner, though may occasionally be restricted by forestry operations. It's also quite popular with mountain bikers. Follow it through the trees and alongside a recently cleared area. Avoid one side path which descends to the right; the correct path runs almost level, curving gradually left to head almost due west. A signed footpath descends to the right; ignore this too and continue along a wider track for almost a kilometre, keeping straight ahead at a junction (reversing part of Walk C10)

Above: Stile in the later stages, looking towards Fair Oak Fell.

until a bridleway crosses the track. Follow the bridleway down a steep grooved descent, continuing across a field then slanting down to a metalled farm track.

Follow this down to a road and turn left. Go left 400m. Just past a house (Weedacre Barn) look for a stile set back on the right under an ash tree. Descend diagonally to another stile then straight down to a third and straight ahead before bearing right at a cattle drinking trough to a gate and road. Turn left for 350m then right on an obvious track (not so obviously, this is the line of a Roman Road). Go past a barn then left into a field and down its left edge. Keep straight on down until the fields run out, where a footbridge hides in foliage on the left. Cross a field, skirting above a steeper bank, to a stile onto a road.

Turn left, then right at a sign 'Little Bowland'. Follow this lane to a right-angled bend where two gates on the left both have footpath signs. Take the right-hand gate and go diagonally right; pass the corner of a fence and continue towards a clump of trees, which hides a pond. Cross stiles just left of this and continue in the same line towards the corner of a wood. (There are currently extra stiles to cross here but they're related to pipeline works and should be temporary). Thread through the rushes, staying right of the wood, to a gate just left of a white house. Follow the boundary wall then bear left along a stream to a footbridge.

Cross and go straight up the field to pass right of a barn and emerge on a lane. Turn left and follow the lane into Chipping. After 600m, there's a section of concessionary bridleway running parallel which gives relief from the tarmac. Drop down to a T-junction on the edge of Chipping and turn right into the village.

L5 Chipping—Garstang

A thoroughly satisfying journey

Distance: 17.3km (10.8 miles)
Ascent: 355m (1,165ft) Descent: 454m (1,490ft)
Minimum time: 4½ hours
Underfoot: A lot of tarmac, but mostly on very quiet lanes, including the estate roads of Bleasdale.
Public transport: Bus 4 Preston–Longridge–Chipping, regular services Monday–Saturday; Longridge also has connections to Clitheroe and Blackburn. Bowland Transit B12 runs between Clitheroe, Chipping and Garstang on Thursdays in summer – one bus each way.
Parking: Car park off Club Lane.
Public toilets: At car park.
Refreshments: No refreshments en route.
Maps: OL41
Start: SD 622 434

Any walk that takes in the perfectly sculpted bowl of Bleasdale is well worth doing and this route threads through it from east to west. That centrepiece is reached by an interesting traverse across the gullied lower slopes of Parlick. After Bleasdale it descends to the hidden mill village of Calder Vale and then makes a final descent to Garstang with the plains of the Fylde and the shimmering expanse of Morecambe Bay spread out below. It feels like you're turning your back on the hills, but if L6 is to follow tomorrow it's only a temporary respite.

The Walk

From the centre of the village walk past the church and turn right up Church Raike. Leave the village then keep left at a fork. Follow the road for over a kilometre. It looks on the map as if you can follow footpaths via After Lee to Fish House and avoid most of the road – but take it from me, you don't want to do this except possibly during a drought.

Keep left at the junction with Fish House Lane, then turn right over a stile. The ground here can be muddy but it's positively arid compared to the After Lee route. Head straight up the rising ground (towards Parlick) then bear left, keeping to grass above a rushy hollow on the left. Cross a stile then follow the fence on the left before bearing right to another stile. Continue to meet a lane near a junction. There are nearly always parked cars here as this is the start of the shortest route to Parlick, popular with walkers and – when the wind is right – with paraglider and hang glider pilots. For a close encounter with the launch sites, see Walk C9.

Go right up the lane a few metres then left over a stile. This field is the favoured landing ground, so stay alert. Head rightwards up the field to another stile (hidden at first but in line with your previous course). Continue along a faint green path, running virtually level across

Opposite: Chipping village scene.

the slope. Cross another stile then rise slightly to a fine stone stile in a wall. Continue level and then down to cross a stream just below a huge gully in the fellside.

Slant down through the fields towards a farm (Blindhurst), bear right along a wall then down left by a signpost to enter the farmyard. Go right through the cobbled yard to a rough track descending into Bleasdale. The track levels out and begins to fade. Bear right to a foot-bridge then up the field to a tarmac track and signpost. Turn left to a small green hut (a bird hide), through a gate alongside, across a field and through a wood. Keep straight ahead to reach a junction of estate roads beside Bleasdale School. Take the road straight ahead, left of the school.

If you've energy to spare, and fancy gaining a bit more altitude, turn right here instead, and shortly you'll pass St Eadmer's Church, where Walk C7 joins in. Follow this up onto the fell and along the rim of the bowl and stick with it until it rejoins the road (Delph Lane). Keep with C7 past Rough Moor farm until it meets another farm track, then turn right down this, rejoining the main route.

Follow this road, keeping straight ahead at each junction. After 1km, crossing a stream, observe the packhorse bridge off to the right. Climb steadily past estate houses and the walled grounds of Bleasdale Tower before the road levels out past another farm (Fell End). As the road swings right, bear left to a small gate under trees and through the narrow plantation to a public road (Delph Lane).

Go left 150m then right (signpost Landskill and Calder Vale Church). Go straight down (high level option rejoins on the way down) to meet a surfaced track. Turn left, swinging right immediately. Go through a farmyard (Landskill: a fine farmhouse with the date 1687 over the

Above: View over Bleasdale to Beacon Fell. Opposite: Garstang Market Cross and Royal Oak pub.

door) and straight ahead down the continuing track. Follow it bending right, over a cattle grid and down left again. Just after another right bend, go left down a steep footpath with lots of steps (these can be very slippery when damp).

Emerging into Calder Vale village, bear left to follow the road over the river and up past the shop and village hall. Pass a second terrace of houses then go right on a footpath up steps and behind houses. Cross a field to a stile then aim right of a white house to a footbridge and a confined path, which leads out to a road.

Go right a few metres then left at a gated stile. Follow the left edge of the field and keep straight ahead over a rise before Garstang finally appears below. Keep following the field edges down then bear left into a farmyard. Cross a stile and descend through a small patch of woodland then rejoin the farm track down to a road.

Bear left (really straight ahead) and then keep right down Parkhead Lane. Pass the entrance to Bramble Wood then keep right down a green track, which crosses the M6, with a stream running alongside. Cross the railway and bear left over a stile and through a field. Turn right along a cutting, fairly obviously the line of an old railway. The line leads easily to a bridge over the River Wyre on the edge of Garstang. The rail embankment has been adapted to act as a sort of dam, used occasionally to impound flood waters. (Very occasionally: I have never actually seen it in use).

This is the line of the Garstang & Knott End Railway, which branched from the West Coast Main Line just south of here. Opened as far as Pilling in 1870, the line was extended to the coast at Knott End in 1908, mainly to service salt extraction there. The salt works closed in 1925 and passenger services ended in 1930. Goods traffic ceased in 1950 and the track was lifted soon after. We can't blame all rail closures on the infamous Dr Beeching.

Cross the river, drop down left, skirt the cricket field and walk through a car park to reach the High Street. South-bound buses go from here; for northbound buses go left down the High Street then turn right by the pie shop on Stoops Weind (just one of several Weinds or alleys in the town); when you emerge to another road the bus stop is just up to the right. The visitor information centre is nearby too, in the new buildings alongside Booth's supermarket.

L6 Garstang—Caton

A grand day out

Distance: 29.6km (18.4 miles)
Ascent: 730m (2,395ft)
Minimum time: 7¾ hours
Underfoot: Be prepared for anything.
Public transport: Garstang has regular buses, including Sunday; 40/41 link Preston and Lancaster, 42 Blackpool–Lancaster. Caton is served by Lune Villager services 80/81/81/81B from Lancaster, half-hourly Monday–Saturday; Sunday service hourly. Mid-route there is a very limited weekday-only service to Abbeystead, but it could be used for emergency bale-out.
Parking: Car park at north end of High Street, Garstang.
Public toilets: At start.
Refreshments: No refreshments en route.
Dogs: The route skirts the edge of a no-dogs area so keep 'em on leads on the fell and in farmland.
Maps: OL41
Start: SD 495 455

This is the longest stage of the tour, and there are limited opportunities to split it either by use of public transport or by an overnight stop. There is no regular accommodation in the middle part the route, and clean water would be a problem for anyone planning to camp or bivouac. That's why this stage is at the end of the tour, so that with luck you will have 'walked yourself in' and be ready for it. Start early, take plenty of water and food, and don't rush, and you should enjoy what is a fitting climax to a week's tour. Its mix of lush valleys, woods, rough moors and rocky ridges with far-reaching views nicely sums up the diversity of Bowland walking. Good transport links make it eminently practical as a standalone walk too.

The Walk

Walk through the car park and skirt the cricket pitch (if you walked from Chipping, retrace the final few steps). Go under the bridge then over an embankment and continue upstream, traversing Garstang's Millennium Green, which is now managed for amenity and wildlife; there can be some very fine shows of wild(ish) flowers in the top field before you emerge onto Wyre Lane.

Turn right then fork left on a narrow path and across a bridge. Turn left up the riverbank, past a pipeline bridge, then climb over a hump and follow a trodden path across fields, parallel to a stream on the left. Turn right a few steps then left into a works yard to a green footbridge over the railway. Join a track curving up and over the motorway and follow it directly away from the mayhem, alongside a wood and out to a lane. Turn left and walk over two fords (both usually dry) before forking right on a bridleway. Follow this, keeping Grizedale Brook on your right, through the lovely valley until the track climbs to the dam of Grizedale Reservoir. Walk beside the reservoir then turn right on a concessionary path, signed to Grizedale Bridge, which skirts the head of the lake and runs through Holme Wood.

Emerging from the wood, cross the beck, go up a few steps then turn right following a bridleway (North Lancashire Bridleway) to a small car park at Grizedale Bridge (start of Walk C5).

Follow the road uphill (as for C5) and away from the bridge, with the high heathery slope on your right and widening views on the left. As the road begins to descend, take a signed footpath on the right. It's narrow but clear enough, curving round the hillside and keeping roughly level. Follow it to a waymark post with arrows pointing straight ahead and left. Turn left. (C5 continues straight ahead).

Turn left, downhill, staying just left of a small stream (Foxhouses Brook). Keep straight ahead to join a farm track, follow down to a junction and turn right; go past Lane Head – a very impressive conversion a la Grand Designs – into a muddy continuation track, running straight until it crosses a stream and forks. The more obvious branch climbs left, but the one to follow is the sunken track that keeps right, emerging beside a ruined house. All this is bridleway, but does not inspire the urge to return with my bike.

Bear left following bridleway markers, go through a shallow ford and continue almost straight ahead to a road.

Go straight across into a tarmac farm track (sign Swainshead). Follow this – an easy kilometre to enjoy the views of Wyresdale – until it loops up into the yard at Swainshead. Bear right in the yard to continue. As the track bends left over a cattle grid, go straight ahead through a gate and down a field to a culvert/bridge in the far corner. Cross the stile then bear left, along a cattle track on slightly higher ground. Pass a fenced-off marshy patch, bear left past a pool and continue down to a corner under trees.

Cross the stile into woodland and descend a steep little path. New plantings and thick bracken make this hard to follow, but keep the steepest ground just to your left and don't cross a wire fence on that side. You should find a lush green track, with one or two waymarks, slanting down right to a footbridge over the River Wyre. If you miss the track don't panic as you'll soon come to the river and only need to scout upstream to find the bridge.

Cross the bridge and go straight ahead to find steps climbing through a wood. Cross a gravel track and continue up with woods on your right. As the slope eases go left over a stile towards farm buildings. Go left of the metal sheds and through the farmyard, with glimpses of a grand house (Lentworth Hall) on the left, to leave on the access track. As this bends back right into a long avenue, go through a gate and keep the same heading through a field to a stile onto a road. Turn right.

Take the next road left, opposite the entrance to Lentworth Hall (you may well wonder why the right of way doesn't simply follow the drive, but it doesn't). Follow the tree-lined lane pleasantly for almost 1km, past two footpaths on the left and one on the right, to a dog-leg where footpath signs point left and right. Go left through a small gate with a carved stone (representing a violet or pansy) alongside.

(NB: some of the fields on the next stretch can be wet and after a spell of really wet weather it may be preferable to follow the lane; turn left, then left again on a busier road to reach Jubilee Tower.)

Go straight up a field and then follow a hedge on your right to pass a farm (Tills Farm). Keep straight ahead on a muddy track and keep following the same line until you reach a narrow squeeze stile in a short wall, with another farm ahead on the skyline. Continue through a much drier field, bear slightly left to a boulder below a sycamore then up the field edge to a track near a house. Almost straight ahead is a stile in a patch of garden.

Follow the left edge of two fields then cross the stream and continue, now with the boundary on your right, to a stile in a corner. Go straight ahead through a rough field, bearing left along power lines towards a house. Skirt the bounding wall and join the access track. Follow it to a junction, turn right and go up past another farm (Westfield House). Jubilee Tower is now visible ahead and there's a rough path direct to it but it's probably easier to follow the farm track to the road then turn right to the tower – or just go straight ahead, across the car park, to continue. Built to mark Queen Victoria's Diamond Jubilee in 1897, Jubilee Tower is a very popular viewpoint but you can feel secretly smug as the views from the fell are vastly wider and better.

Go past an Access Area sign and follow the path to a footbridge over the first stream. The way to Grit Fell is clear, with a fence just to the right the whole way, but in most conditions occasional improvisations are needed to avoid wet patches. Overall, though, it's a pleasant steady climb.

Grit Fell begins to earn its name as the path steepens before spilling onto a boulder-strewn plateau. The prominent stile at a meeting of fences is not the true highest point, but might as well be. The surveyed summit is about 60m due south, but hardly worth the bother. The path doesn't even visit it while the most prominent cairn is clearly not at the highest point.

Without crossing the stile (unless you really must find the summit), turn left along the fence. Cross a smaller stile and follow a path, variously stony and peaty, along the broad ridge (so broad it hardly merits the term) for about 400m. Look for a narrow but distinct path going off right from a dip in the main path, and follow this (now reversing Walk C1) to meet a 4x4 track near a wrinkled outcrop. Go straight across and continue down the narrow path, soon running in or alongside an obvious groove. Pass several old grouse butts before the path levels out and goes vague crossing a marshy area. Keep slightly left to descend near a stream with some nice little cascades, then follow more grooved tracks down into a little hanging valley (see Walk C1 for notes).

Turn right to a stile (leaving C1) and follow an obvious terraced track level then down. At a T-junction of tracks turn right, cross a stream and follow the fence before crossing at a stile.

Opposite: Descending into Brookhouse, with the Lune Valley beyond.

Go down a muddy track, cross a footbridge and follow the track straight ahead until it bends left to a farm. Go through gates left of a barn and continue into the access lane. Follow this winding down steeply and then more gently into Littledale.

Meet a road and keep right (really straight ahead); cross a bridge and go up past a Scout camp. At the next junction go straight ahead up a track, soon becoming rough. Meet a road again and go straight down for 1km. At a right-hand bend there are two footpath signs close together, both with metal kissing gates.

Use the second stile. Connect two more stiles and keep straight ahead over a rise and down to another stile where a hedge meets a fence.

Go down a line of thorn trees and a few steps left to a metal kissing gate. Go down to another kissing gate and an enclosed path leading to streets. Go straight ahead to meet a main road.

The centre of Brookhouse and the Black Bull pub are 500m right, but the nearest bus stop is about 150m left. To continue into Caton, and complete the circuit of Bowland, continue past the bus stop another 600m.

Brookhouse was originally Caton. The area around the church and pub was the original centre of the village; until the 19th century, what we now call Caton was a relatively small settlement known as Town End. The development of a turnpike road (now the A683) and the opening of the railway in 1849 – with a station at Caton – meant that Town End grew faster than the parent village. Eventually an agreement between the Post Office and County Council meant that 'Town End' became Caton and 'Caton' became Brookhouse.

And if that's not enough, when you reach the A683 in Caton, go straight ahead down the short road left of the Post Office then turn left on the cycle-path which runs, via Crook o'Lune, all the way into Lancaster.

Road Bike Rides

Bowland has some great biking roads, which attract riders from all over Lancashire, and far beyond. It will be no surprise that there are some tough climbs, but that's what gears are for. Travelling these roads adds to a fully rounded appreciation of the area, and it's hardly worth debating that cycling is the best way to do so. You'll feel the country with all your senses in a way that motorists never can.

For those who are not regular cyclists, the prospects may appear daunting. Of course it's not compulsory to cycle these routes at all, but they are so rewarding! It would be asking a lot to leap straight in to a route like Bowland Knotts and Cross o'Greet (R7) with its 1,000 metres of ascent; much better to start with the Lune Valley (R1) or Wenning and Hindburn (R2).

Bikes

It's not compulsory to do these on a pure road bike, though it makes it easier. Any decent hybrid will do well enough; a genuine mountain bike might be slightly harder work, though swapping knobbly tyres for semi-slick ones will make a big difference to speed on the road. Effective brakes are essential for safety, especially here: many of the routes involve descents which can be long, steep or both. Nick o'Pendle is the prime example. When the gradient tilts the other way, it's the range of gears that makes all the difference. With the right gears, and maybe after a few warm-up rides, anyone fit enough to handle the walks in this book should also be able to manage the bike rides.

Of course you can walk up the climbs but this is actually harder work (oh yes it is) as well as slowing you down drastically. It's no disgrace, of course, to push occasionally (e.g. on the last bit of the ascent to Cross o'Greet) but if you regularly find yourself walking, look hard at the range of gears on your bike. It is often possible to extend the range without replacing the entire bike: new sprockets and/or chainrings may do the trick – ask in a good bike shop. The other crucial factor for efficient pedalling and enjoyment is fit. Not how fit you are, but whether the bike is the right size and correctly set up. For example, many people are riding with saddles too low, greatly reducing pedalling efficiency and risking long-term injury to their knees. Again, a decent bike shop should be able to help you; if you're buying a new bike they should certainly do several checks to ensure the sizing and setup are correct. A real bike shop will also help you check your position on your existing bike. With luck, they won't even charge for this, especially if you spend a few quid on other essentials such as new tyres – but if they did, it would be money well spent. Getting a perfect fit is a complex process but you can get most of the way in three simple steps.

First, make sure that the bike itself – specifically, the frame – is the right size. If the saddle is right down on the top tube, for example, then either it's too low or the frame is too big. Second, get the saddle position right – height first, then the fore-and-aft setting. A correctly set saddle both raises pedalling efficiency and greatly reduces the risks of problems with knees or hips. As a first approximation, your leg should be slightly – but only slightly! – flexed at the bottom of the pedal stroke. Check the fore-and-aft position with the cranks horizontal: you should then be able to drop a plumb line from your kneecap to the pedal spindle (on the leading leg!). Third, get the handlebars set right. This improves control as well as comfort, and reduces problems with back, shoulders or neck. Handlebars and/or stem can be replaced without breaking the bank, and the dividends can be great.

Maps

Navigating on roads is inherently easier than on the fells, so not carrying a map at all is an obvious option. However, a map could come in handy should you ever need to 'bale out' for some reason. A map also helps set the route in context and settle arguments about the identification of distant landmarks. Unless you're desperate to save every last gram, I think it's worth carrying one.

OS Landranger maps are more than adequate for road cycling. Unfortunately the Landranger sheets do not cover this area neatly, and several are needed to ensure complete coverage of some rides. The best map for road cycling in Bowland is the Harvey Forest of Bowland for walkers, cyclists and horseriders, which conveniently covers the entire area at a useful 1:55,000 scale. The only bit of riding not covered is the link from Lancaster (R1 bonus) but this is easily followed without a map.

Timings

Timings for bike rides are much more variable than for walks. It's a reasonable benchmark that most people will walk at around 3mph/5kph on the flat; there's no such 'average' figure for the bike. Professionals racing on closed roads could conceivably average around 40kph/25mph on these road loops. I've based my timings on a much slower average speed (less than half as fast), but this still assumes a reasonably fit rider, a decent bike with appropriate range of gears and, crucially, that you ride up all the climbs. If you're unsure, allow plenty of extra daylight to complete the first few rides until you have a better benchmark.

Above: Ringstones Lane, seen on ride R2 with Ingleborough behind.

Ride R1 Lune Valley

Sweet cycling dreams are made of this

Distance: 28.2km (17.5 miles)
Ascent: 610m (2,000ft)
Minimum time: 1¾ hours
Roads: Mostly quiet, and mostly on good surfaces, but there's a gated minor road, which is uneven in places. Some long steady climbs, and some short steep ones too.
Public transport: No direct access but the route can easily be linked to Lancaster main line station via the Lune cycle-path (see end of section).
Parking: Crook O'Lune car park.
Public toilets: At Crook O'Lune car park.
Refreshments: No refreshments en route.
Start: SD 522 647

If you want to be pedantic, this is more of a ride around the Lune valley than actually in it, since it largely avoids the busy A683 which is the main and in some places only road through the valley itself. The penalty, of course, is that it is significantly hillier than a pure valley ride would be, but the wide, often changing and frequently excellent views are a more than adequate reward.

The route first explores the rolling green hills north of the Lune before an obvious chance for a mid-ride break in Hornby. It then climbs onto the higher, wilder hills on the northern fringe of Bowland proper, delving into Roeburndale before making a fine exit on one of the

least-known roads in the area. After that it's all downhill, in the best possible way.

The Ride

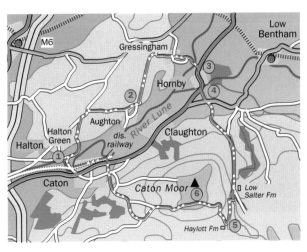

1. Exit the car park and turn right – take care as this stretch can be busy. Turn right on a bend and ride past Halton Park, a fine old manor house, before a short steep climb. Continue to a T-junction. Turn right on a busier road then first right off it, signed for Aughton. Continue along the road with some fine views of the Lune valley and the Yorkshire hills soon appearing. The road skirts above the main part of Aughton (pronounced Affton) village; if you want to explore this quiet backwater a short loop road drops down on the right and rejoins further on. Continue to a T-junction and turn right.

Aughton is principally known for its Famous Aughton Pudding Festival, traditionally held every 21 years. At the last one, in 1992, the villagers produced a world-record plum pudding weighing 3.28 tons. Very tasty it was too. Whether they're planning to go one better in 2013 remains to be seen.

2. Descend into Gressingham, running out past the church onto the floodplain of the Lune. Cross the beautiful triple-arched Loyn Bridge with care, as it's quite narrow and other traffic may try and bully through or past; there are two refuges on the way across. Loyn is an old spelling of Lune and the bridge is thought to date from the late 16th or early 17th century. Just above as the road bends right are a World War II pillbox and above that the Norman motte and bailey of Castle Stede – possibly the best such site in Lancashire. Continue along the straight road to meet the A683 on the outskirts of Hornby.

3. Keep straight ahead (technically a right turn) on the main road and drop down into the village, with pubs and shops making it the obvious place for a mid-ride break. Among notable buildings in Hornby are the octagonal-towered church of St Margaret – it also has an unusual polygonal apse at the east end. Crossing the bridge over the Wenning, Hornby Castle is conspicuous on the left. Most of the visible structure is Victorian or later, but it's built around a mediaeval core.

As the main road bends right at the end of the main street, keep straight ahead on Station

Opposite: Near the end of the big climb out of Roeburndale

Road, then go straight over a cross-roads (B6480) into Moor Lane, and immediately start to climb.

4. The climbing continues in stages for about 3km before levelling out on moorland overlooking Roeburndale (start of Walk C17). Follow the road on a steepening descent to Barkin Bridge and climb out the other side, then fork right through a gateway (North Lancashire Bridleway sign). This barely feels like a public road, but it is.

Descend again to cross the River Roeburn then climb quite steeply before levelling off approaching a farm (Haylot).

5. Just before the farm turn sharp right and soon descend again to cross a stream (Bladder Stone Beck). A gate near the bridge means at least one person has to make a standing start on the steep climb out. Continue more easily to another gate and T-junction and turn left. (From Hornby to here is the same as MTB ride M4). Keep climbing gradually for another kilometre or so before cresting out with the valley of Littledale appearing below and left.

6. Descend for several kilometres, rattling over two cattle grids. Keep straight ahead at a fork and twist through a dip before resuming the descent. At an angled T-junction bear right on a slightly busier road and descend for another couple of kilometres into Brookhouse. At a T-junction turn right and immediately left (if the Black Bull doesn't delay you) into a narrow road (Holme Lane) and follow this down to the A683. Go straight across and in a few metres meet the Lune cycle-path. Turn left and it leads back to Crook o'Lune.

Link from Lancaster
6.2km (3.9 miles)
Ascent: Virtually flat
Leave Lancaster station by the exit on Platform 1 and follow the cycle track alongside a sports field, with the ground of Lancaster City FC adjacent. The ground is called Giant Axe, apparently not after any prehistoric finds but simply because of the shape of the field as seen on a map. Exit onto a road, turn right to go under the railway and then immediately left onto another cycle-track. Follow this past the striking Millennium Bridge and then come up slightly to almost meet a busy road before wriggling right and back left into an underpass. Continue along the cycle-track to Crook o'Lune.

Above: Topping out on the climb above Halton park; Clougha Pike is very distinctive on the skyline.
Opposite: Climbing onto the moors, with Ingleborough behind.

Ride R2 Wenning and Hindburn

A little gem: so good you could go round twice

Distance: 22.3km (13.9 miles)
Ascent: 415m (1,360ft)
Minimum time: 1½ hours
Roads: Generally quiet lanes with reasonable surfaces: a somewhat busier road near the end.
Public transport: 5 trains daily to Wennington (4 on Sundays) (Leeds–Lancaster/Morecambe line).
Parking: The small car park at Wennington station is officially for rail users only so park considerately nearby.
Public toilets: None.
Refreshments: Bridge House Farm and pubs in Wray, Bridge Inn, Tatham.
Start: SD 617 699

At the risk of flogging a cliché, this ride is small but perfectly formed; it's hard to think of any way to improve it except maybe by making it a bit longer. But hey, there's a place for short rides – and it's not too easy. There's scarcely a flat section except for bits of Mewith Lane and the kilometre or so from Wray to the Tatham Bridge.

The climbs don't just add a measure of challenge; they also take the route out onto open slopes with terrific views across into Yorkshire and then over the Lune valley to the more

distant Lakeland skyline. I'm not kidding when I say a second lap is a real temptation.

The Ride

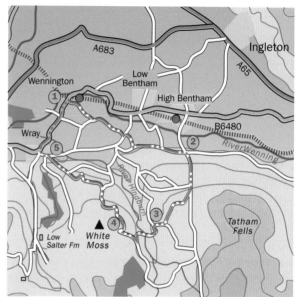

1. Turn left out of the car park and left again (Old Moor Road) to climb over the railway and continue steeply for a few minutes. It should get you warmed up, anyway. Level out, keep left, and follow the lane more easily, keeping left at the next junction. Continue to a T-junction, turn left and almost immediately right (Cross Road). At the next T-junction turn left; this is Mewith Lane, which is followed for about 3km to a crossroads.

2. Turn right and start climbing again. It's steepish at first, then eases off as the road emerges onto open moor, with great views especially to the left. Pass the small parking area which serves the Great Stone of Fourstones (start of walk C18) then take the second road on the right, Ringstones Lane. Climb a little more then descend, with a steep twisting dip and rise through a wooded valley. At a sort of T-junction on a bend turn right and descend some more to a T-junction at Ivah.

3. Turn left and after a few more twists and turns cross the river Hindburn (Stairend Bridge). Make a steep shady climb out then, still in the woods, take the first road on the right. Climb some more before emerging into open surroundings. There's another steep bit then a more gradual ascent to the high point of the ride at White Moss.

4. Coast down now, on a quiet lane with great views over the Lune valley with the Lake District fells beyond. However, beware of low-flying sheep along here: we genuinely had a near miss where the road runs below a steep bank. Several cattle grids later, keep straight on at a junction. The gentle tone of the descent is broken by a steeper, twisting section through woods but soon resumes. Keep left again at the next junction and soon make a steeper descent into Wray, with a T-junction right at the bottom.

5. Directly opposite is Bridge House Farm, with its excellent tea room. Turn left and ride through the village (shop and pub) to another T-junction. Turn right on the B6480. This is busier but it's not much over 2km back to Wennington. If there's still time to kill before your train, the Bridge Inn (usually known as the Tatham Bridge) is about three minutes ride from the station.

Approaching the turn onto Ringstones Lane.

Ride R3 Brock, Bleasdale and Harrisend

Keeps getting better and better

Distance: 33.8km (21 miles)
Ascent: 465m (1,525ft)
Minimum time: 1¾ hours
Roads: Mostly quiet, with generally good but not silky-smooth surfaces. Higher Lane is narrower and rougher and a smoother alternative is suggested.
Parking: On the road just south of the village centre.
Public toilets: Pay toilets by road just south of Scorton.
Refreshments: The Barn and The Priory in Scorton
Start: SD 503 487

If you've read the walks descriptions you'll know I rate Bleasdale as a very special bit of scenery, and this route finds an excellent approach, climbing gradually around the flanks of Beacon Fell before circling through Bleasdale itself. If that's not enough for one ride, there's the climb (a bit less gradual in places) onto Harrisend Fell, yielding far-reaching views before you plunge into what is – sheep permitting – one of the best descents in the area. It's becoming clear why Scorton is a favourite destination for cyclists.

This route does coincide with R4 for a fair distance, but it's hard to see an alternative and these roads are so good who's going to complain?

The Ride

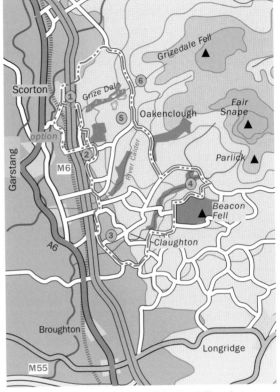

1. Roll down the main street heading south out of the village; pass the Anglican church with its prominent spire then turn left on Tithebarn Lane*. This is mostly uphill, getting steeper at the top.

Turn right at a T-junction (Higher Lane) and soon descend steeply to a ford (usually dry). Climb again and continue to another T-junction; turn left and climb very steeply then turn right a further T-junction (Eidsforth Lane).

Follow the lane down to another angled junction; continue straight ahead and level.

*Riders on very light tyres may find Higher Lane a bit rough: it can be avoided by staying on the main road instead of turning up Tithebarn Lane. After 1.5km turn left on Hazlehead Lane. Follow this over the motorway and up past Shireshead Church to rejoin the main route at point 2.

2. Follow the road past several side turnings to a T-junction on a bend; bear right. At the next junction, not far from the motorway, bear left (almost straight ahead) on Sandholme Lane. Follow this past a couple more side roads until you reach a junction with a triangle of grass, again within earshot of the M6. Bear left, on a long straight parallel to the motorway, swinging away from it at the next junction.

3. Follow the road for almost 3km, crossing the little River Brock en route. Rise to a T-junction and turn left, with signs for Longridge. Climb a sharp rise then take the next left on Scotch Green Lane.

Follow this road past several side turnings, climbing steadily most of the way. It changes name to Bleasdale Road. Beacon Fell starts to loom a bit menacingly ahead but the road soon

Opposite: Top of the steep section on Delph Lane.

sidles off to the left. Keep following the road, spurning all side turnings, until the climbing finally ends (for a while, anyway) on a rise lined by pine trees, where grand views of Parlick and Bleasdale unfold on the left.

4. Descend through a couple of sharp bends then take the next turning left (Bleasdale Lane, signs for Garstang). Follow this with a couple of sharp drops followed by equally sharp rises where it pays to be alert with the gear-shifters.

After a level stretch turn right on Delph Lane. This drags up steadily then throws in a steep section just to finish you off. It may be worth taking a breather at the top to enjoy the expansive views that have opened up unsuspected behind you (Walk 7 starts here). Continue along the level crest then swoop down into Oakenclough. The former mill buildings here now house a range of enterprises – one of which, until a police raid in 2009, was the growing of cannabis!

5. Follow the road round right (but watch for cars at the junction at the bottom, as some drivers seem unable to comprehend how fast you may be travelling). It's nice to carry plenty of speed into the next rise, which shouldn't be too painful. Level out alongside Grizedale Lea Reservoir then dive down to Grizedale Bridge (start of Walk 5). Again, it's really sweet to carry as much speed as possible into the rise on the other side.

6. This is the last climb on the ride so it's nice to make it a good one. This road was used on the 2007 Tour of Britain, when Mark Cavendish was seen in an unusual role in a long two-man breakaway. The first part of the descent is sweeping and open but watch out for sheep. After a cattle grid it gets steep, with a sharp bend at the bottom. At the next crossroads turn left on Long Lane (signs for Scorton and Garstang). Follow the lane, mostly descending, and passing all side turnings, finally crossing the M6 and rolling back into Scorton.

Above: Scorton is perennially popular with cyclists.Opposite: The Marshaw Wyre near Tower Lodge

Ride R4 Chipping—Oakenclough—Trough of Bowland

An absolute classic, and not as tough as you might expect

Distance: 44.6km (27.7 miles)
Ascent: 765m (2,510ft)
Minimum time: 3 hours
Roads: Mix of narrow lanes and wider minor roads with generally decent surfaces.
Parking: Car park off Club Lane just west of the church. This has public toilets so it's a useful reference point even if you don't arrive by car – and is directly behind the Cobbled Corner Café, which might be even more useful!
Public toilets: At car park in Chipping, and in Dunsop Bridge.
Refreshments: If you start in Chipping the first regular refreshment stop is Dunsop Bridge. There's also a snack-wagon at Langden Brook most weekends and daily in summer.
Start: SD 622 434

The Trough of Bowland is well known both generally, and specifically in bike racing history. This narrow pass through the hills has been used for many centuries, perhaps most notoriously as the route by which the Pendle Witches were conveyed to trial and execution in Lancaster. The road on the steep eastern side is certainly one of the most spectacular in Lancashire. It may come as some relief that the west side, the approach used on this ride, is considerably less steep, but the route makes up for it with several other respectable climbs, including Harrisend Fell and the final crescendo from Burholme Bridge. These may be the highlights, but the riding is good throughout and the scenery, though ever-changing, is pretty continuously superb.

The Ride

1. Exit the car park and turn right, away from the village centre. Follow the winding road, ignoring all side turnings, and following occasional signs for Garstang and Inglewhite. After about 4km you pass the Bowland Gliding Club and the steep triangular face of Parlick looms above; when the wind is right this is usually confettied with hang gliders (see Walk 9). Swing left, descend to a tricky double bend and continue another 1km to a right turn signed for Bleasdale, Oakenclough and Garstang.

2. Drop down to Higher Brock Mill and tackle a sharp climb out again. This is soon followed by another steep drop to Jack Anderton Bridge – try and carry good speed for the rise the other side. (The route here coincides with Ride R3 for a while).

After 2km turn right on Delph Lane, signed Oakenclough and Lancaster. There's a steady drag of a climb followed by a much steeper section. Enjoy the views as the road levels out over Rough Moor then swoop down to the industrial hamlet of Oakenclough; keep round to the right at the junction.

3. A modest rise leads to a fast descent to Grizedale Bridge, but watch out for the cattle grid near the bottom – it's easy to hit this at an angle, and it's very slippery when wet.

If you aren't balked by cars you should have plenty of speed to 'fly' the next rise, topping out at 176m on Harrisend Fell. This climb has been used several times in the professional Tour of Britain and, as you're about to discover, it's considerably steeper on its north side. As the descent levels out, turn right at a crossroads, signed Marshaw and Trough of Bowland. Follow a leafy lane with many twists and dips – keeping a good rhythm here is an enjoyable challenge. After a final straight ascent the road swings left and levels out, with grand views over Wyresdale (Walk 3) to Ward's Stone (Walk 2) and Wolfhole Crag (Walk 4). Make a pleasant descent in a little side valley before a very steep (20%) climb out at Cam Brow. It wouldn't be so bad if the run-in were straight but there's a nasty hairpin at the bottom to scrub off all your speed.

4. Keep right at the next junction and ease down the moors to the River Wyre. Turn right at a T-junction after a short rise and ride past Marshaw and Tower Lodge (start of Walk 4); the shade of the tall pine trees along here is welcome on hot days and it's a very popular picnic spot. As the trees end the road rises more steeply but – assuming a sensible range of gears – it's still mostly a sit-down climb, with only three or four shortish sections demanding stand-on-the pedals assault. The road levels out and crosses a cattle grid, the summit of the Trough of Bowland.

It's worth pausing here a moment, or at least easing off. An obvious large milestone marks the old county boundary – yes, this was once the entry into Yorkshire, and no, they can't have it back. Below it are two small memorials. One honours Bill Bradley, winner of the Milk Race (precursor of the Tour of Britain) in 1959 and 1960.

The 1959 Milk Race included a fearsome, and now legendary, stage across the Pennines – in fact, across the entire country, from Whitley Bay to Morecambe – won by Bill Bradley. Some riders finished well over an hour behind. A stalwart of the South-

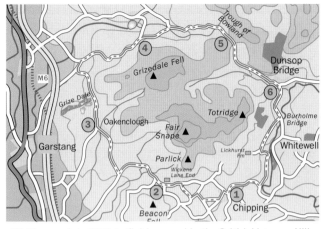

port Cycling Club, Bill was still fit enough in 1985 to finish second in the British Veterans Hill Climb Championship.

The Trough climb has featured in professional and amateur races many times since; it was last included in the Tour of Britain in 2006.

5. The descent is steep and twisting, with some blind spots – take care. Lower down it all opens out magnificently and given a clear road you can really build up some speed. Roll on past Sykes Farm and the parking places at Langden Brook; there's often a tea-wagon here but I prefer to keep the momentum for the sharp rise just beyond. It's then an easy run down to the outskirts of Dunsop Bridge, passing the Village Hall, where teas are available on summer Sundays. (The route here coincides with Ride M2). Just beyond is a junction on a bend; bear right (or turn left into the village for Puddleducks tearoom or the public toilets).

6. Follow the level valley road for 2.5km then turn right just before Burholme Bridge (signed for Bowland Wild Boar Park) and begin the final climb of the circuit. It's a long gradual drag followed by a steep section right at the top – a true sting in the tail. Sweep down and continue past a dead-end road by a red phone box. About 100m further on, M2 goes right but though the route here looks innocent (smoother than the road in fact) it soon reverts to mountain-bike territory. Follow the road past the entrance to the Wild Boar Park; there's a nice tea room here but it's at the bottom of a lengthy drive, which you would then have to climb back up.

7. Keep descending until the road wraps round Wardsley farm and climbs a short rise. Keep right at the junction above and keep following the lane back into Chipping. At a T-junction turn right along the main street back to the start.

Ride R5 Bashall Eaves—Marl Hill—Harrop Fell—Holden

A real surprise package

Distance: 39km (24.2 miles)
Ascent: 610m (2,000ft)
Minimum time: 2 hours
Roads: Some remarkably quiet roads, generally good surfaces. Busier near the end.
Public transport: Train to Clitheroe.
Parking: Car park on Chester Avenue, behind the station.
Public toilets: Near Council Offices in Clitheroe.
Refreshments: Backridge Farm, Bashall Barn and Red Pump Inn early in the ride; string of pubs near the end, but nothing in the middle without an awkward detour into Newton or Slaidburn.
Start: SD 742 419

The obvious route through the Hodder valley via Dunsop Bridge, Newton and Slaidburn is just that – obvious. So much so that most people (cyclists and motorists alike) completely overlook the 'by-pass' in the sweet little side-valley of Easington Brook. Well, don't tell the motorists, because we wouldn't want to spoil it. This lovely stretch of road is bracketed by two fine climbs – actually, the second one isn't that much of a climb, but you do get two absolutely cracking descents.

One climb but two descents? This sounds like cheating, but that's how it feels. And to be fair the first climb is not to be underestimated, with a long drag through Bashall Eaves before it gets more serious on the way to Browsholme Height. It's never vicious, though, and then the rewards just keep on coming.

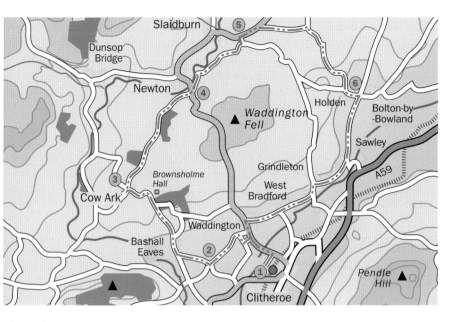

The Ride

1. From the station (platform 1), turn left and left again under the railway then bear right and ride past the car park (from the car park, just turn left) and ride along the street to a T-junction; turn left, and this too is Waddington Road (B6478).

Follow the road across the Ribble and into the outskirts of Waddington village. Turn first left (Waddow View), right at a T-junction (Edisford Road) and then left at the next (Twitter Lane). Follow this out of the village and you'll soon find yourself riding along a low ridge with views in all directions. There are refreshment opportunities at Backridge Farm and Bashall Barn – both excellent, but it's a bit early in the ride.

2. Drop down after Bashall Barn to a triangular T-junction and bear right. The road begins to climb, gently at first, past the Red Pump Inn and through the small village of Bashall Eaves. Keep climbing pretty steadily until you pass the entrance to Browsholme Hall. The road swings left and levels out then dips to a sharp bend at Cow Ark. Just after this bend turn right and in 200m turn right again.

3. Now the climbing gets a bit stiffer, though it's never really precipitous. Still, by the time you top out on Browsholme Height, you've gained almost 250m in altitude since the start and your legs will probably know all about it. Swoop down between plantations into a dip and

Opposite: The Ribble and Pendle Hill, near Sawley.

power up the other side to Marl Hill (Walk C12 crosses here). Now the real descent starts, and it's a cracker, with a long straight run followed by some gentle curves. However, the head-down bum-up attitude may be best for speed but isn't fully compatible with enjoying the views. The road sweeps round and rolls to a T-junction (the B4678 again). Watch out for speeding cars as you turn left for 50m then go right into a quiet and narrow lane.

4. Follow this most pleasurably through the little hanging valley of Easington Brook, parallel to the main Hodder valley, which lies hidden beyond the low ridge on the left. Using this route reduces distance and saves a stiff climb out of Slaidburn, as well as being much quieter than the B6478 through Newton. However it does miss out on the refreshments available in both Newton (pub) and Slaidburn (pub, café and shop). Swings and roundabouts...Crossing Walk L3, the lane climbs out of the valley and up to a junction opposite a small plantation.

5. Turn left here, then right at a T-junction, briefly joining the B6478. However, leave it at the first opportunity, forking right after 400m (Tinkler's Lane); the lane climbs a bit more, in a rolling sort of way, before bearing right and making up its mind that it's time to descend. This is another belter, with no nasty bends and some great views to Pendle Hill. It finally levels out by the little hamlet of Holden and coasts to a T-junction beside a pub (Copy Nook Inn). (Walk C15 uses the level bit of this road).

6. Turn right and follow this somewhat busier road for 3km. Just before it reaches a bridge over the Ribble, turn right, signed for Grindleton.

The bridge would quickly take you into Sawley, where there's the Spread Eagle pub as well as the picturesque remains of the Cistercian abbey.

Villages (and pubs!) come thick and fast now. Follow the road into Grindleton (Duke of York), where it bends left and descends. Keep right at the next junction to continue to West Bradford (3 Millstones). Keep straight ahead through the village and the road leads in about 1.5km to Waddington, where there are several pubs and a tea room. Turn left down the main street (B6478 again) and follow it, soon rejoining the outward route, back into Clitheroe.

Above: Descent after Bashall Barn, with Longridge Fell beyond. Opposite: Descending towards the cross-roads which takes you towards Downham.

Ride R6 Tour de Pendle Hill

Packs a lot into a short distance

Distance: 30.1km (18.7 miles)
Ascent: 740m (2,430ft)
Minimum time: 2 hours
Roads: Urban at start and end, otherwise mostly minor roads with generally good surface.
Public transport: Train to Clitheroe.
Parking: Car park on Chester Avenue, behind the station. Those with cars could also start from Barley and omit the link to/from Clitheroe.
Public toilets: Near Council Offices in Clitheroe; at car park in Downham.
Refreshments: Lots of opportunities in Sabden, Newchurch, Barley, Downham and Worston, plus the Clarion House on Sundays and Bank Holidays.
Start: SD 742 419

Nick o'Pendle is probably the most famous cycling climb in Lancashire. This ride does it the easy way, but it's still not to be sneezed at. Over the top you're pitched abruptly into the Forest of Pendle, with its dark associations of witch hunting. The climb out of Sabden is the steepest of the day; after that you can relax a bit though there's still the more gradual ascent out of Barley in store. The road then sweeps grandly around the shoulder of Pendle Hill before dropping into Downham then sidling out on one of the best Quiet Lanes in the district. If you get round this in under two hours you can really call yourself a cyclist – though with so many pub stops, and spots for admiring the view, it's just as much fun to take all day over it.

The Ride

1. Negotiate the mini-roundabout opposite the station, and ride up King Street. Turn left at the top (Castle Street) and then in front of the lovely wedge-shaped Library turn right down Wellgate. At the end turn right on busy Waterloo Road (A671) and then first left into Shaw Bridge Road, which leads on into Pendle Road. Follow this through a roundabout and continue to meet the fast and busy A59. Fortunately our acquaintance with this is brief. Cross carefully (or it may be even briefer!) using the signed cycle route via the central reserve, and escape hastily into a lane almost opposite, signed for Sabden.

2. Follow this road, climbing steadily. Pass the turning for Pendleton (any relation to Olympic sprint champion Victoria Pendleton?) and, higher up, the small dry-ski slope of the Pendle Ski Club. Continue up the moorland road to top out quite suddenly in the narrow pass of Nick o'Pendle. You can descend considerably quicker, but watch out as the hill spits you abruptly into the streets of Sabden. Ride straight ahead through the village, and all too soon you're climbing again; at the top of the street fork left (signed Padiham) and crunch up another steep climb.

Nick of Pendle or (as I have always thought) Nick o'Pendle? The usually reliable OS maps have the former version but locally the latter is almost always preferred. By either name, this is a famous climb in bike racing, but we're doing it the easy way. As we see on the descent, the south side is considerably steeper: 25% at one point. It's been used many times in races like the Tour of Britain and its forerunner, the Milk Race, as well as for many standalone hill climb events. In 1988 Chris Boardman (better known for Olympic track exploits and Tour de France prologue wins) won the national championship on this hill. In 1980 the winner was Malcolm Elliott, who was still racing professionally in 2010 at the age of 49. The course record is around 3½ minutes (I haven't been able to confirm the exact figures). I once rode it in less than twice that!

3. At the top is a crossroads (signed Barley and Newchurch). Turn left and ride along the near level ridge with great views over the valley of Sabden Brook and up to Pendle Hill – this is the heart of 'Witch Country'. Keep straight ahead to a T-junction and turn left (signed Newchurch). Descend into the valley and then climb again. The lane swings right and into Newchurch. The church isn't new now, with most of its structure dated to phases of rebuilding between 1653 and 1740. (Postdating the infamous witch trial of 1612). An unusual feature is a curious oval opening on the west face of the tower, known as the Eye of God.

4. The normal route now would be to keep left and climb steeply out of the village, soon dropping down into Barley, but on Sundays and some Bank Holidays a short detour is really worthwhile to step into cycling and social history. For this, turn right just before Witches Galore (Jinny Lane) and in just under 1km pass the entrance to Clarion House.

The Clarion movement sprang from a newspaper of the same name, founded in Manchester in 1891, and quickly established a wide following for its principles of co-operation, community and fellowship. Associated clubs also developed, including cycling and rambling clubs, especially in the great northern industrial towns. The National Clarion Cycling Club, founded in 1895, is still going strong. This particular Clarion House was built in 1912 and is still run on a non-profit basis. On its open days it serves famous mugs of tea, other drinks (non-alcoholic)

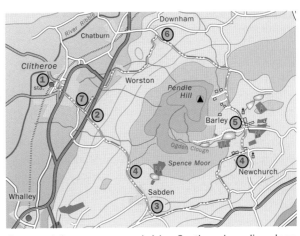

and confectionery, and you're welcome to bring your own sandwiches Continue down Jinny Lane to a T-junction and turn left. Ride into Barley where the shorter route rejoins.

5. Continue through the village, passing the handsome Pendle Inn on your left. Leaving the village, begin the last major climb of the route, rising steadily onto a shoulder of Pendle Hill. The line of the main ascent route can easily be seen slanting up the steep face of the hill (Walk C14 uses this). Continue more easily to a crossroads and turn left. The road swoops scenically round the flanks of the hill and then dives straight down into Downham. To explore this celebrated village properly (or visit the pub!) you'll need to continue up the hill to the church. However the route itself turns left just before the road crosses the stream: this has signs for NCN 91 (Lancashire Cycleway) and is designated a Quiet Lane – pretty well merited in my experience.

6. Follow the lane up a short climb and skirt south of the abrupt Worsaw Hill, a geological oddity – a Waulsortian Mudmound, no less. Descend into the little village of Worston and another possible pub-stop. As you leave the village, fork left to avoid the nearby A59. Follow the narrow lane until it meets the main road, then bear left along the cycle-path until it ends at an obvious crossing-point. Cross to another narrow lane parallel to the A59 and follow this to a crossroads*.

7. Turn right and follow the road back into Clitheroe. Note that the upper part of Wellgate is one-way so follow the arrows round into Lowergate then turn right up King Lane and straight across into King Street.

*If you started from a parked car in Barley, turn left here, and pick up the story at the first crossing of the A59 (Point 2).

Ride R7 Bowland Knotts and Cross o'Greet

A treat for the climbers, a fabulous challenge for the rest of us

Distance: 45.6km (28.3 miles)
Ascent: 995m (3,265ft)
Minimum time: 3 hours
Roads: Minor roads throughout; mostly good surfaces but beware of wandering sheep on descents.
Public transport: Rail station at High Bentham (Clapham is also close to the route).
Parking: You can avoid the dip into/out of Bentham by parking where the road first reaches open moor: roll back down to the crossroads/garage and turn right onto Mewith Lane.
Public toilets: At the car park in Slaidburn.
Refreshments: Pub and café in Slaidburn
Start: SD 668 690

One look at the figure for total ascent tells you that this is a seriously hilly ride, crossing the main spine of the Bowland Fells not once but twice. Unless you're very confident, get some of the other routes under your belt first; like the Grand Traverse for walkers, this is one to aspire to. And also like the Grand Traverse, when you're ready for it, it is a magnificent day out. Big climbs promise two things: big views and grand descents, and this loop delivers handsomely on both counts.

Tackling the route in the described direction is probably slightly kinder, but there's not much in it and it's extremely rewarding either way.

The Ride

1. From the railway station turn right (Station Road) and follow the road over the river (Wenning) and straight on up the hill. After 1.5 km, at a crossroads with a garage, turn left on Mewith Lane. Follow the lane, undulating but generally keeping around the same contour, for nearly 6km; it changes name several times though you're unlikely to notice. Just avoid all side turnings until you reach a crossroads in the middle of open moor, shortly after passing the little chapel at Keasden.

2. Turn right here. It's not long before the lane starts to climb, and it then does so very steadily, with long straights where the way ahead is laid out before you. It steepens a bit near the top, but never too viciously. Roll over the cattle-grid on Bowland Knotts at 422m, just a few metres lower than the return climb at Cross o'Greet.

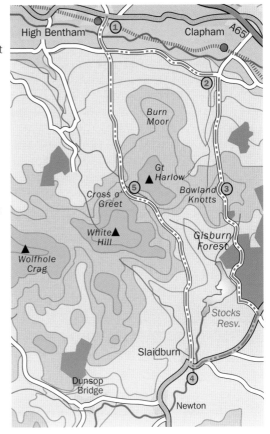

3. Sweep down across the moor, with some steeper drops and a couple of bends before the road enters Gisburn Forest. There are some very sharp bends here and there can be traffic (including walkers and mountain bikers) emerging unexpectedly from side turnings, so please be vigilant.

Roll past Stocks Reservoir and climb a little to pass Dalehead Church; pass the Cocklet Hill car park (main start for the mountain bike routes) before leaving the forest behind. Climb to a crossroads, turn right and follow the B6478 along an open ridge and then down (one hairpin bend) into Slaidburn, the obvious refuelling stop.

Dalehead Church was built in 1937, using stone from the original Dalehead Church which was demolished when Stocks Reservoir was built, flooding the village of Stocks-in Bowland. It's not used for regular services but does double duty as a wayside chapel and a heritage

Opposite: Riding past Stocks Reservoir.

centre with visual displays about the history of the valley. The churchyard is also a Biological Heritage Site where over 130 species have been recorded including several types of orchid.

4. Ride up the main street and turn right by the fine war-memorial. Soon the road climbs again, steadily up to the crest of Merrybent Hill, which offers fine views over the Forest and back south towards Pendle Hill. Negotiate some sharp bends and rise again, then drop down past a plantation to a bridge (Cross o'Greet Bridge). The road starts to rise again immediately, scratching its way across a steep rocky fellside. As the valley closes in, the road is funnelled towards the headwaters of the Hodder. The top is near but a couple of steeper pitches rear up before you finally roll out at 427m and – weather permitting – a huge view to north and east explodes around you. This is truly a great moment and worth savouring. It's also worth considering putting an extra layer on, or emulating the Tour de France traditions and stuffing

a newspaper up the front of your jersey. You'll be warm from the climb but it's nearly all downhill from here and speed chills.

5. The descent has a steep start then lots of long straights. It should be possible to carry plenty of speed to make light work of the occasional dips that interrupt the downward career. A final long open straight whisks past the Great Stone of Fourstones (see Walk C18).

Descend more steeply to the cross-roads with Mewith Lane; keep straight on, now retracing the outward route, into Bentham.

Above Bentham, with view of Whernside (rider travelling opposite direction to that described).

Mountain Bike Rides

Let's be clear: all the routes described here are real mountain bike rides; some stretches on all of them are definitely more challenging than your average canal towpath or former railway track. That's not to say that they are for hardcore devotees only; anyone who's reasonably at home on a bike can tackle most of these rides provided they have a suitable bike (see below) and are prepared to walk for short sections if necessary. The one exception to this is the harder of the two routes in Gisburn Forest, which really does demand some previous mountain bike experience.

Apart (again) from Gisburn's purpose-built red trail, none of these routes will entirely satisfy the hard core rider. They are much more about exploring the area on a bike, with the rougher bits of trail coming as an entertaining bonus. If in doubt about either yourself or your bike, M1 is certainly the best route to start with.

There are many other tracks and trails in Bowland which would appear ideal for biking, including dozens of kilometres of shooters' tracks and estate roads. However, at the moment these are not rights of way for bikes. It is a sore point that the Right to Roam, in England and Wales, added absolutely nothing to the rights of bikers – unlike Scotland, where bikers have essentially the same rights as walkers. In some cases negotiations are ongoing to try and secure access agreements – using these routes illicitly is only likely to jeopardise such discussions. Equally ironically, there are a number of bridleways shown on the map which are physically unsuitable for biking or simply don't fit into a suitable circuit.

There are one or two venues in the AONB where 'unofficial' trails appear to be sanctioned, or at least tolerated, by the landowner. This delicate balance may only last while usage remains local and low-key so I've refrained from including them but here's a hint: if you did all the walks in this book you would get a good idea about at least two of them.

One very easy ride that families could enjoy is the tarmac bridleway up Whitendale, starting just west of the bridge in Dunsop Bridge. After about 3km it crosses the river near a small waterworks and an information point. Shortly after that it splits and the left branch can be taken for another kilometre or so to Brennand House, but after that it becomes more hardcore.

It is about the bike

It's worth repeating: these are real mountain bike rides. By extension, therefore, they should be tackled on a real mountain bike.

But what is a real mountain bike? This is actually quite hard to pin down. It's usually taken to mean a bike with fairly chunky frame and wheels, knobbly tyres plus suspension at front and maybe at the rear too – oh yes, and lots of gears. However, there are people riding trails like these on bikes with a single gear and no suspension at all.

The awkward fact is that there is no simple definition of a mountain bike; it's more about fitness for purpose than wheel size or number of gears. Factors like frame angles and riding position (a complex business usually summed up under the heading geometry) are crucial. Many hybrid or leisure bikes may look superficially like a mountain bike but a 'sit-up-and-beg' riding position – ideal for towpath cruising – makes them less stable and harder to control on trickier trails.

Having said that, almost any bike can be made at least a little more trail-friendly by the simplest of upgrades: a change of tyres. But you can't fit knobbly MTB tyres on a slinky road frame: the wheel sizes are different and there is unlikely to be enough room for the fatter tyre. It's definitely a case of consult the bike shop first.

If you want to ride off-road regularly, and enjoy it to the max, then a real mountain bike is a sound investment. Sadly, real mountain bikes don't come cheap. Realistically the minimum spend for a new adult mountain bike is £300. There are lots of cheaper bikes that look the part (superficially) but are far too heavy, making them a pain on climbs and killing any real agility on the trail. They may have flaky geometry and won't last long on rough terrain.

For £300, or even £500, there's no point in even considering a full-suspension bike. In any case the ideal first mountain bike is a hardtail, i.e. a bike with suspension fork out front but rigid rear end. A hardtail will be lighter than a 'full-sus', have better fittings for the same money, be easier to maintain and more versatile for riding on roads or easier tracks.

Kids' Bikes

Most kids' 'mountain bikes' are a disaster; cheap full-suspension bikes with dodgy components and equally dodgy geometry. Often as not, they are actually heavier than a half-decent adult bike. This is, of course, totally the wrong way round. Kids are not only lighter than adults but also less strong in proportion to their weight. However, because they are lighter, kids have less need for suspension on a bike. The best mountain bikes, especially for younger kids, are specifically designed for off-road riding but may have no suspension at all. Of course it may be hard to persuade the youngsters of this when all their mates are flaunting the bling of full suspension, but the proof is in the riding.

Bike Hire

The best way to get the measure of mountain bikes and mountain biking is to borrow or hire a bike before splashing the cash. For bike hire centres in the area see listings at the back of the book.

Jargon buster

Mountain biking has a language of its own. We've already met hardtail, full-sus and geometry. Here are just a few more terms that should prove useful in reading the route descriptions here.
Singletrack (always one word, not two): a trail that's only wide enough for one rider at a time. May sometimes be little wider than the tyre itself. Mountain bike Nirvana for many.
Freeride: where mountain biking meets the skate park. Riding for fun rather than to cover a distance, with an emphasis on jumps and other obstacles.

North Shore: timber boardwalks and other elevated sections. Can be extremely alarming, but the only example here is a not-so-scary stretch on Gisburn's Red route.

Technical: trail that demands developed riding skills.

Berm: big banked curve, usually manmade and designed to be ridden at speed.

Timings

Even more than on the road bike rides, timings for mountain bike rides are extremely variable. It's possible to find yourself pushing not only uphill but in places downhill and on the flat too. The timings, however, assume that you can ride pretty much everything on the route.

Maps

You shouldn't need a map at all for the waymarked trails in Gisburn Forest and route finding should be straightforward on the other routes too. But a map is always a handy back-up and if you're going to carry one it might as well be a good one. When you venture off-road, a 1:25,000 scale map is ideal for navigation, and all the rides are fully covered on OS Explorer OL41. The Harvey 1:25,000 map is less useful, with full coverage only of the Gisburn Forest trails (though not the optional link from Tosside).

Ride M1 Caton Moor

Have fun

Distance: 16.3km (10.1 miles)
Ascent: 494m (1,620ft)
Minimum time: 1½ hours
Underwheel: Mostly lanes, some rougher tracks with some quite steep loose sections on the main descent.
Public transport: Nearest rail station: Wennington (4.3km to Point 2).
Parking: Beside the bridge in Hornby.
Public toilets: None.
Refreshments: No refreshments en route.
Start: SD 585 683

Less technical than M2, this is a great introduction to Bowland mountain biking – or even to mountain biking in general. Most of the climbing is on tarmac and is amply rewarded with fantastic views. The descents are absorbing but not too difficult. I'm tempted to say it could be tackled on something less than a full-on mountain bike, but then where do you draw the line? You might not need suspension but you definitely need knobbly tyres, effective brakes and a good range of gears.

The Ride

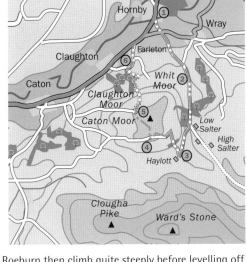

1. Turn right out of the car park. As the main road bends right at the end of the main street, keep straight ahead on Station Road, then go straight over a crossroads (B6480) into Moor Lane, and immediately start to climb. The climbing continues in stages for about 3km before levelling out on moorland overlooking Roeburndale (start of Walk C17).

2. Follow the road on a steepening descent to Barkin Bridge and climb out the other side, then fork right through a gateway (North Lancashire Bridleway sign). This barely feels like a public road, but it is. Descend again to cross the River Roeburn then climb quite steeply before levelling off approaching a farm (Haylot).

3. Just before the farm turn sharp right and soon descend again to cross a stream (Bladder Stone Beck). A gate near the bridge means at least one person has to make a standing start on the steep climb out. Continue more easily to another gate and T-junction and turn left. (From Hornby to here is common with ride R1). Just before a cattle grid at almost the highest point of the road, turn right onto a rough (and fairly new) track

4. This seems quite a tough climb though there's only about another 30m of height to be gained. As you level out, two things compete for your attention: the massive pylons of the nearby windfarm and the tremendous panorama of Morecambe Bay and the Lakeland fells. Roll on down to a gate where you meet another track.

Opposite: Track past the windfarm on Caton Moor. Above: Descending through the tress below the clay workings.

5. Bear right and ride, roughly level at first, past a house (Moorcock Hall); long a skeletal ruin, it's now being restored. Descend a gritty track with fine views up the Lune valley and twist down to a bridge near the clay workings which serve the Claughton brickworks; you pass under the cableway which transports the clay. The operation was mothballed in 2010. Follow the track round left and enjoy an exciting descent, with some fairly steep sections and intermittently loose surface. After a slight rise join a surfaced track, which runs straight, down the hill. Claughton Hall stands high on the left; it originally stood in the valley, on the outskirts of Claughton village, but was demolished and rebuilt on its present site in the 1970s. The track soon turns rough again. Watch out for a junction just above the village where another track goes sharply back right; if you pass any houses you've overshot.

6. Follow this track until it runs straight out into a lane in the little village of Farleton; continue to meet the A683 and turn right. The main road is unavoidable here, but it's only about 1km back to the outskirts of Hornby.

Shortly after joining the A683, on a left-hand bend, you pass the old Toll House (white with overhanging eaves). This bit of road has a modest claim to fame as the first place in the world to have white lines painted on the road. Around 1922, John Willacy – owner of a garage that stood next to the Toll House – painted lines on his own initiative after a number of accidents had occurred on the bend. It seems 'the authorities' objected and Mr Willacy appealed to King George V. The Ministry of Transport finally approved the use of white lines in 1925.

Above: Descending after Moorcock Hall, with views up the Lune Valley. Opposite: Track across the moor before the descent to Lickhurst

Ride M2 Chipping–Dunsop Bridge and back

Some cracking trails in delightful surroundings

Distance: 22.5km (14 miles)
Ascent: 515m (1,690ft)
Minimum time: 2 hours
Underwheel: About 1km of fairly technical singletrack; otherwise easy tracks and lanes.
Public transport: Nearest rail station: Clitheroe (14km).
Parking: Car park off Club Lane.
Public toilets: At car park
Refreshments: Tea room at Dunsop Bridge (slight detour); pubs and cafés in Chipping.
Start: SD 622 434

For any true mountain-biker, the undoubted highlight of this route is the lovely trail along the valley side below Totridge; both technically intricate and scenically perfect, its only failing is that it isn't longer. But this may be its saving grace for those with less relish for the rough stuff; it's perfectly feasible to walk the tricky bits here, while still enjoying its delightful position. The rest of the route – apart from two very short sections at fords – is either much easier trails or lanes. Adjust your expectations accordingly.

Note: Looking at the map, a more obvious route out of Chipping would appear to be following the North Lancashire Bridleway from the start, via Chipping Lawn and Park Gate. However, this may be fine on horseback but isn't on a bike, with a difficult ford followed by a grinding climb on long moorland grass with no discernible track. Take the described route instead, which uses very quiet lanes and a good track.

The Ride

1. Ride up the lane left of the church to a fork on the edge of the village (as for Walk C9). Go down and right past factory buildings new and old, pass a mill pond, keep right at a junction, and continue to the end of the public road (about 3km). Tarmac continues straight ahead but there's a wide entrance on the right (possibly with a few parked cars) which funnels into a rougher track.

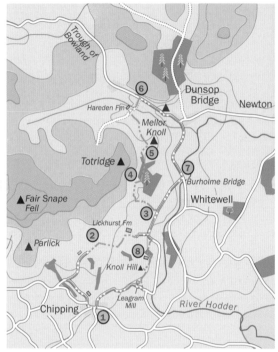

2. Follow this track, soon dipping to a gate just above a ford; there are stepping stones on the left if you don't fancy the watery route. There's a steep climb from the ford, gradually easing onto open moor; the track is always obvious. Follow it over the top, with very promising views ahead, then descend, swinging right, to a farm (Lickhurst). Bear left through the yard and join a narrow tarmac lane; this runs through a sweet little valley and carries virtually no traffic. Follow the lane to a sort of crossroads (the road on the left is private) near a red phone box.

3. Continue straight ahead on a slightly busier road and follow it for about 1km, mostly climbing. Go over the top, with grand views of the Hodder valley, and very soon bear left on a tarmac track with bridleway sign. Follow this as it climbs then bears left to cross a ridge of abrupt limestone knolls. At a junction turn right and descend a bit. As the track swings left, turn right on a rougher track between henhouses and follow it around the hill to a gate at the corner of a plantation.

4. Now the fun starts. Follow the singletrack trail along the edge of the trees then bear left through the forest, climbing most of the way, to another gate at the far side.
The trail descends and then undulates along the hillside through fine tall beech trees. It's beautiful but mostly you need to keep your eyes on the trail ahead as it's quite technically challenging in places – probably more so than anything on the regular red trail in Gisburn

Forest. Eventually the trail climbs to another gate then follows an indefinite line across a field, still climbing gradually. Continue to a gate in the angle of a wall, on the saddle between Totridge and Mellor Knoll.

5. Bear slightly right; again the line is a bit vague but soon becomes clearer, swinging left as the track starts to descend. Go through another gate and continue down. When the track becomes indistinct again, bear slightly right and aim for the left end of a small wood just below. Pick up a clear track once more and follow it down to a farm (Hareden). Bear right through the yard and follow the tarmac track out to a road.

6. Turn right and follow the road. Shortly after crossing a cattle grid there's a bridleway sign on the left, but one glance shows that there's no real track, just a tough mix of grass, sedge and rushes. It's much easier to stay with the road to a T-junction on a bend. If you need refreshment, the shop and tea room in Dunsop Bridge are just a short way down to the left, but to continue the ride bear right (effectively straight ahead). This road is busier, but it's flat and easy, and we'll only be with it for a little over 2km. Turn right at a triangular junction onto a narrow lane (signs for Bowland Wild Boar Park).

7. The lane soon begins climbing; just before the top you'll recognise the bridleway you took earlier, so self-evidently the next bit is ground you've already covered. Keep straight on and descend back to the crossroads by the red phone box, but now follow the road round left. In another 200m turn right on the track (bridleway) to Higher Greystoneley. Follow the track straight through the yard; it now gets rougher and descends through woodland to an obvious ford. This is quite slippery and the concrete exit ramp can be even more so: I've seen walkers take a tumble here, never mind bikes, so assess the conditions carefully. Continue up more easily, soon reaching another farmyard (Lower Greystoneley).

8. Go straight ahead and continue along a much easier track. There's a slight climb to round the quarried outcrop of Knot Hill, then the track descends to meet a lane. Turn right and follow the lane for about 2km into Chipping. A bit more than half-way along, there's a stretch of permitted bridleway through a belt of woodland parallel to the road; this can easily be followed for a last bit of pleasurable off-road stuff before rejoining the lane for the final descent into the village. Turn right at a T-junction for the village centre and car park.

Above: The little valley below Lickhurst.

Ride M3 Gisburn Forest Trails

Bowland's very own Coed y Brenin

Distance: Bottoms Beck trail 8km (5 miles), The '8' 18km (11.2 miles)
Ascent: Bottoms Beck trail 240m (790ft), The '8' 380m (1,245ft)
Minimum time: Bottoms Beck trail 1 hour, The '8' 2 hours
Underwheel: Mostly forest track and good gritty singletrack on the Bottoms Beck trail: the '8'
adds rocks, North Shore, big berms and all manner of amusement.
Public transport: Nearest rail station: Long Preston (11.3km to Cocklet Hill).
Parking: Cocklet Hill car park (the first one reached on the southern approach to Gisburn
Forest). This now regularly fills to capacity so please note that it is also easy to join the trails a
little further on, parking either where the road widens as it crosses a small dam/causeway, or
at the Vicarage Garden car park a little further on. Join the trails immediately north of the
dam or at a wider gate about 150m further north (see also Walk C16).
The forest can also be reached quite easily from Tosside on the B6478, where the Dog and
Partridge pub has branched out with the Whelp Stone Café. It also has a bike-wash facility.
(The easiest route from Tosside to the forest is along Bailey Lane: keep straight ahead on
entering the forest to meet the '8' before the quarry.)
Public toilets: Currently nothing on site but rumours that some provision will be made in the future.
Refreshments: Van at Cocklet Hill on most weekends, otherwise no refreshments en route.
Start: SD 746 549

Anyone who knew the cycle trails in Gisburn Forest a few years ago is in for a big surprise. A substantial injection of cash and a concerted effort by an alliance of professional trail-builders and local volunteers has resulted in development of a really significant new set of singletrack trails; they're already at least on a par with better-known sites like Grizedale Forest in the Lakes (better in my view), and there's a promise of more to be added.

The two main routes are the '8', graded red, and the blue-graded Bottoms Beck Trail. If you're not sure what to expect, try the blue route first and if you find that well within your compass, you should be able to ride most, though maybe not all, of the red.

Note: The forest roads can be ridden in either direction but the dedicated singletrack sections are strictly one-way only; be sure to follow the waymarks. As the routes are extremely well waymarked there's no need for detailed instructions, so what follows is just a general indication of what to expect.

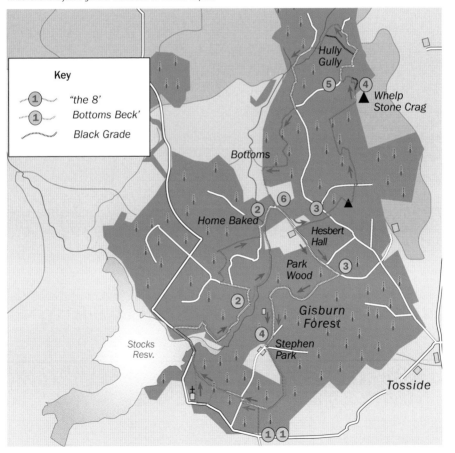

Opposite: An alternative route around the rock steps Overleaf: Relaxing singletrack at the end of the farther loop of the 8

The '8' (Red)

This does indeed form a crumpled figure-of-eight on the map, with the two loops linked by a short section of forest road near Hesbert Hall (which is therefore ridden twice). This also means that keen riders can do repeat laps on either loop, and that the southern half can be ridden on its own for a short visit – it's also more sheltered in poor weather.

1. Red and blue routes share the first section from Cocklet Hill, making for a relatively mellow start – ideal for a warm up. The routes briefly split before the descent to the causeway, then continue together along the first section of the track known as Eggberry Road (see Walk C16). Watch out for the next divergence (marker post 14) where the '8' goes left into the forest: this section is short and mostly climbing. A bit more fire road and then there's a longer section of singletrack, volunteer-built and known as Home Baked, twisting through the trees, sometimes with little room to spare, and making an absorbing descent back into the valley.

2. Climb on fire road, swinging right, and ride past Hesbert Hall. The short way back to the car park is straight ahead but the second loop swings left and climbs some more. The top of this climb is a good place for a breather, both because the views have really opened out at last and because what follows is a more continuous and intense stretch of singletrack.

3. Very shortly, the route swings through an old quarry (long used as a semi-official freeride venue), crosses a rock bridge (exciting but not really difficult) and gets stuck into the tricky, twisting climb of Sheep Hill. This is followed by a lengthy North Shore section; again it's exciting rather than really technical as the chunky, rough-hewn timbers give great grip even when wet.

More open sections follow as the trail keeps climbing, with some rocky sections, before finally topping out on a shoulder just below Whelpstone Crag (visited on Walk C16).

4. There are some chunky rock steps here – intimidating but straightforward – and a foretaste

of things to come with some big swoopy berms. This area's so good the trail ties itself in knots trying to stay high for as long as possible, and there's an extra black-graded loop for the more advanced riders, which includes a very steep slab/drop. Sweep down through some more berms to a forest road.

5. There's another black-graded option just ahead in the form of Hully Gully, while the regular red trail takes a longer route mostly on

Above: Intimidating but straightforward rock steps below Whelpstone Crag

fire road but with a nice singletrack link at Dob Dale (some will remember this as one of the pre-existing singletrack sections). Then there's more fire road before another pre-existing singletrack stretch, which starts easily but gets more interesting on the steep rooty descent to Thorp Syke and the equally steep climb out. The old straight track down to Bottoms has been overlaid with a series of berms; these need to be ridden with confidence as the marly soil is very slippery when wet (and it dries slowly under the trees). An easier trail along the valley leads to déjà vu as it meets the linking section.

6. This time keep straight ahead after Hesbert Hall. From here on the red and blue routes share the same trails (for now anyway), but it's by no means dull with some nice valley-side singletrack and some sweeping berms. More advanced riders may want to take these at speed, but be aware that there may be novices taking a more tentative approach just ahead.

Bottoms Beck Trail (Blue)

This blue-graded trail makes a great introduction to real mountain biking; there's certainly a lot more to it than monotonous forest roads.

1. The first section from Cocklet Hill is common with the red trail, then the blue takes a more circuitous route through the forest before the descent to the causeway. The Eggberry Road track is wide but bumpy and then the route runs through an obvious cutting, once used by a railway built to ferry stone from quarries higher up the hill for construction of the dam (the red route visits one of these quarries and several others are shown on the OS map).

2. The trail runs pleasantly along the valley of Bottoms Beck then rejoins the red route and climbs on forest roads to pass Hesbert Hall.

3. On the descent there's a stretch of genuine singletrack contouring the slopes above Hesbert Hall Syke and Bottoms Beck.

4. Enjoy a grand finale with a long series of big berms before the final roll-out to Cocklet Hill.

There are also miles of forest road which can be freely ridden and pose no technical difficulty. It's probably still possible to follow the old purple-waymarked route around these but why not get hold of a trail map (download from:
http://www.forestry.gov.uk/pdf/Gisburnguide.pdf/$FILE/Gisburnguide.pdf
You could then make up your own route? (It's not as easy as you might think to follow the forest roads from the OS map).

Ride M4 Salter Fell

Two for the price of one – and either way, a tough but terrific day out

Distance: For the out-and-back ride, 42km (26.1 miles)
Ascent: 885m (2,900ft)
For the circuit: 50.2km (31.2 miles)
Ascent: 1110m (3,610ft)
Minimum time: 4 hours
Underwheel: Some lanes; the track itself has grassy and sandy sections but mostly has a compact stony surface.
Nearest rail station: For the out-and-back ride, Wennington. For the circuit: High Bentham
Parking: For the out-and-back ride, park considerately in Wennington; it's also possible to shorten the ride by parking in Roeburndale (e.g. as for Walk C17). For the circuit: Park in High Bentham or shorten the ride slightly by parking on the moor, e.g. in the parking bay for Great Stone of Fourstones (as for Walk C18); lots of other roadside opportunities nearby.
Public toilets: Slaidburn
Refreshments: For the out-and-back ride, Wennington and Wray; for the circuit, also High Bentham and Slaidburn.
Start: SD 617 699 (Wennington); or 668 690 (High Bentham).

This is a tough one. I don't mean the ride itself, though it's certainly challenging (just take a look at those figures for total ascent). Before you even get to that there's a real conundrum about how best to tackle it. The Salter Fell Track itself is a brilliant ride on a good, or even half-decent, day, but there's no legal way to make a circuit out of it without riding at least twice as far on roads as off them. It's not that they're bad roads, either, but they're so much more enjoyable on a road bike, and in fact ride R7 uses most of them.

For maximum off-road enjoyment the thing to do is ride
the Track itself from end to
end and then turn round and
ride straight back again.
There's nothing boring about
this as the character of the
riding feels different in the
other direction and the views
which unfold before you are
quite different too. The only
snag is that there's no chance
of mid-ride refreshment unless
you drop down considerably
further from the end of the
track – and of course you then
have to climb back up again.
It's easier to carry some energy
bars, or go the whole hog and
cart sandwiches and a flask;
there are plenty of great spots
for a picnic.

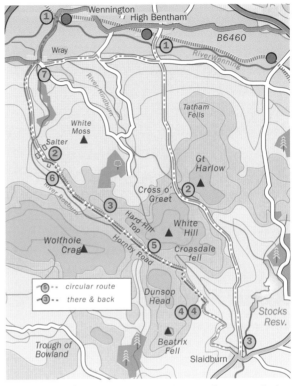

Of course the next ques-
tion is which end to start from
(or which way round if you're planning a circuit). Again it's a toss-up but purely on practical
grounds I'll start from the north as this allows the extra option of access by train. However, it's
a personal choice and if you have your own transport it's equally easy to start from Slaidburn.
My personal preference would also be to get the bulk of the road riding out of the way before
reaping the rewards on the track.

The Route: Out and Back

1. From Wennington station turn left along the B6480 to Wray. Turn left down Main Street
then right up School Lane. Continue up to a T-junction and go left; climb a little more then
level out as you pass a small plantation (start of Walk C17, recommended parking place).
Follow the lane, with attractive views over Roeburndale; look for the pale scratch of the Salter
Fell Track climbing the fells beyond. Descend steeply to a bridge (Barkin Bridge) and climb
equally steeply the other side. Continue along the lane to its end at High Salter Farm.

Opposite: A level section halfway through the climb (north to south).

2. An obvious track continues from the public road, bending left out of the farmyard. Notice the North Lancashire Bridleway markers and a sign stating that it's 18km to Slaidburn. The track climbs fairly steadily, with a grassy surface at first giving way to a mix of rocky and sandy track later on. (For more detail see Walk L2).

3. After a gate there's a more level stretch with views over Whitendale, then a little more climbing (easy now) to another gate at roughly the highest point (416m). The track begins to descend and soon twists steeply down (loose in places) past the remains of old quarries. Keep following the track down, ignoring any branches: the main route is always obvious. Finally go through another gate onto tarmac at the start of a public road (start/finish of Walk C13; possible parking place if starting this end).

4. Turn round and ride back.

The Route: Circular

1. From High Bentham station turn right (Station Road) and follow the road over the river (Wenning) and straight on up the hill (as for R7). After 1.5 km, at a crossroads with a garage, R7 goes left but we go straight on, climbing steadily before emerging onto open moor. Pass

Above: Descending above upper Whitendale (south to north).

the Great Stone of Fourstones (start of Walk C18) and keep straight on. There's a bit of a dip in the greener surroundings of Croasdale before serious climbing resumes, getting steeper near the top; it's a tough haul to the summit at Cross o'Greet.

2. The descent beyond is excellent, again steepest near the top then easing out along the slopes above the young River Hodder. Watch out for wandering sheep, though. Hope for a clear run at the bridge at the bottom (Cross o'Greet Bridge), as momentum helps with the sharp rise just beyond. There's a slight pause then another steepish pull up to the crest of Merrybent Hill. Now there's another fine descent into Slaidburn.

3. Entering the village, at the T-junction by the war-memorial, turn right to continue the ride; (public toilets and tea-room will be found by turning left). Keep straight ahead as the main road bends left: you'll pass the village shop on your left and the Hark to Bounty pub on your right. Follow this lane, mostly climbing, for about 2km to a junction. Turn right (sign for Myttons Farm Crafts) and keep following the lane to its end at a gate.

4. Go straight through; this is the start of the Salter Fell Track. Follow it without navigational difficulty; keep straight ahead where a spur track goes right and soon tackle the steep loose climb past some old quarries. Continue more easily to the summit, go through a gate and begin the descent.

5. In fact it's relatively level for the first couple of km, nicely poised above upper Whitendale. Then the real descent starts, with magnificent views to distract you from the trail itself. There's no real technical difficulty and the track is almost straight, so it's possible to build up quite a speed if you feel like it.

6. At High Salter roll out through the farmyard onto a lane and keep straight ahead through the sharp dip at Barkin Bridge and then along the level moorland road above Roeburndale. Cross a cattle grid and soon bear right (sign for Wray). Descend into the village and turn right on Main Street (it's possible to 'escape' to Wennington station by turning left, then right at the end).

7. As you leave the village Bridge House Farm is an obvious and excellent refreshment stop. Continue along the valley road; after about 1km the road makes a sharp left bend into the scattered hamlet of Mill Houses. Follow the main road round right and up a sneaky little climb. Continue more easily along a nice little ridge. At the next junction turn right (signs for Lowgill and Slaidburn) then first left (Mewith Lane). Follow this for about 3.5km, passing several junctions, to a crossroads with a garage, which you should recognise from the outward journey. Turn left to descend back to High Bentham.

A late finish on the upper slopes of Cross o'Greet (clockwise circuit).

Sources of information

General information
www.forestofbowland.com
Tourist information (accommodation, food and drink)
www.forestofbowland.com/visit_staying
accommodation listings

Tourist Information Centres
Clitheroe TIC
Church Walk, Clitheroe, Lancashire, BB7 2RA
Tel: 01200 425566
email: tourism@visitribblevalley.co.uk

Lancaster Visitor Information Centre
The Storey Creative Industries Centre, Meeting House Lane, Lancaster, LA1 1TH
Tel: 01524 582394
email: lancastervic@lancaster.gov.uk

Garstang Discovery Centre
Cherestanc Square, Garstang, Lancashire
Tel: 01995 602125
email: garstangtic@wyrebc.gov.uk

Settle
Town Hall, Cheapside, Settle, BD24 9EJ
Tel: 01729 825192
email: settle@ytbtic.co.uk

High Bentham Tourist Information Point (April - September)
Town Hall, Station Road, Bentham, Lancaster, LA2 7LH
Tel: 015242 62549
email: tip@benthamtowncouncil.co.uk

Travel and Transport
For general travel information contact one of the above TICs or visit:
www.forestofbowland.com/visit_travel
www.countrygoer.org/bowland.html

Rail Travel:
For timetables and online booking, see:
www.thetrainline.com
Services are provided by two main companies:
Virgin Trains (West Coast Main Line, stations at Preston and Lancaster): www.virgintrains.co.uk/
Northern Rail (other services encircling the Forest of Bowland, stations at Wennington, Bentham, Clapham, Giggleswick, Settle, Clitheroe and Whalley): www.northernrail.org

Maps
Ordnance Survey: www.ordnancesurvey.co.uk
Harvey Maps: www.harveymaps.co.uk
Maps are available at all good bookshops and outdoor gear shops

Outdoor Gear & Hire Shops

Outdoor Gear Shops

Ultimate Outdoors
17 New Street
Lancaster
LA1 1EG
01524 66610
www.ultimateoutdoors.co.uk

Cave & Crag
Market Place
Settle
N Yorks
BD24 9ED
01729 878121
www.cave-crag.co.uk

Onward & Outward
32 King Street
Clitheroe
BB7 2EP
01200 429977
www.onward-outward.co.uk

Whalley Warm and Dry
The White House Stables
82 King Street
Whalley
BB7 9SN
01254 822220
www.whalleyoutdoor.co.uk

Bike Shops

The Edge Cycleworks
2 Chapel Street
Lancaster
LA1 1NZ
01524 840800
www.theedgecycleworks.com

Leisure Lakes Bikes
103 Penny Street
Lancaster
LA1 1XN
01524 844 389
www.leisurelakesbikes.com

Pedal Power Clitheroe
17 Waddington Road
Clitheroe
Lancashire
BB7 2HJ
01200 422066
www.pedalpowerclitheroe.co.uk

Pendle Cycles Padiham
10–16 Church Street
Padiham
Lancashire
BB12 8HG
Tel: 01282 778487
www.pendlecyclespadiham.co.uk

Bike Hire

Pedal Power Clitheroe (see above)

Cycle Adventure
No shop: they'll deliver and collect at most points in the area.
07518 373 409
www.cycle-adventure.co.uk

Photographic Supplies (and advice)

GL Robertson
15 Brock St
Lancaster
LA1 1UR
01524 32045
www.glrobertson.co.uk